AF358663

Create Your Own Website

Create Your Own Website

Learn Web Design
with HTML & CSS

Robin Krambröckers

Create Your Own Website
Learn Web Design with HTML & CSS

ISBN: 9782492280009 Hardcover
9782492280016 Ebook - EPUB

Image sources: Pexels / Pixabay / Robin Krambröckers

CONTENT

INTRODUCTION

WHAT YOU WILL LEARN

20 years ago websites looked like a toddler learning to write. They were entirely made of HTML and text and they were only designed for a desktop computer. Today websites look much more professional. You can even access them from your television. In this book you will create a site that looks like the picture on the right. Keep in mind that you can change everything you want. Not only the title and the images, but also the position of your images and elements.

By the end of this book, you will be able to:

- Create your own website
- Personalize the website
- Design a mobile and user friendly interface
- Access the website from your mobile phone

Preview the site at 'robinkbr.com/demo'.

How to use this book

There are six action chapters. Each chapter covers a theoretical part and an action part. Your job is to work through the chapters and implement the new skills you will learn. At the end you will get a mobile and desktop friendly site. You will be able to show it to your friends, colleagues and associates, every time you have an internet connection.

What do you need?

- A laptop / PC
- A mobile phone
- An internet connection

Some Basics

In the following chapters, the programming languages HTML and CSS are explained. These are the basic elements for the creation of a professional website.

Before we dive right into the code it is important to clarify how people access the web in order to shed light on some terminology.

The World Wide Web (www) is not the internet. The internet is simply the way computers connect to each other. In the late 60's it was created under the name of ARPANET and its main purpose was to create a network between American universities.

Back then computers were big machines in massive rooms not small objects we keep in our pockets.

Later on the internet graduated to the NSFNET (National Science Foundation Network) which connected all universities together to a bigger network.

In the 90's the NSFNET became the internet which connected to commercial networks as well as research networks.

When you connect to the internet, you become a part of a large group of computers.

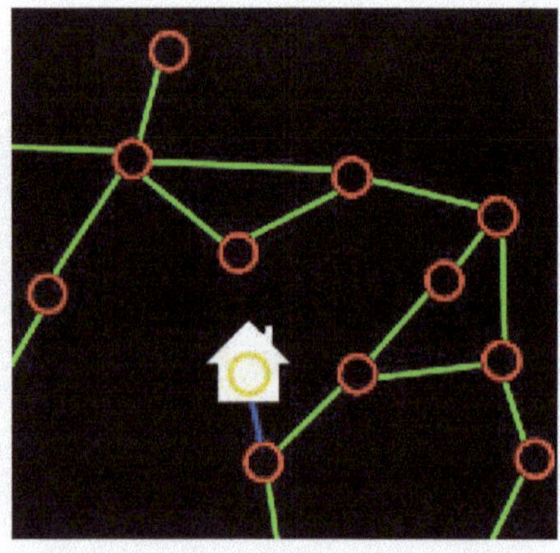

The internet carries a vast range of information resources and services such as email, telephony, file sharing and the World Wide Web.

The World Wide Web is the software, or the program, that runs on the internet. It is mainly used to access Interlinked Hypertext Documents (HTML documents) and web applications also called websites.

How websites are created

To navigate the Web, you use browsers like Chrome, Safari, Explorer or Firefox. They treat the HTML and CSS information and display the websites you see.

Since the creation of the Web, there have been several versions of HTML and CSS. The latest versions are the ones we will focus on in this book. These include HTML5 and CSS3. They cover the older and newer versions. In other words, you can create the older and newer websites if you choose to do so.

GETTING STARTED

1.

GETTING STARTED

In order to build your first website you need to learn *HTML*. It stands for *Hypertext Markup Language*. That is what browsers use to display websites. With this language you can add text and images to your site. You also use it to group pieces of information into lines, paragraphs or sections.

HTML is called a *Markup Language* because it surrounds every piece of content with two *tags*. The first one at the beginning of your content and the last one at the end. They create the effect of a markup on every single piece of content you create.

Before you begin, there are 3 steps you must complete to be prepared.

STEP 1

To begin coding, you will need what is called an *HTML editor*.

This program allows you to create and edit *HTML* files. You could just use the normal pre-installed text-editor of your computer, but it wouldn't show you the mistakes you make.

Even a small error in your code can make it useless. The editor you will download shows you every error and saves you from having to search for hours after a small mistake.

Suggested editors:

- Brackets
- Notepad++
- Visual Studio Code

I recommend you using *Brackets*. Since it is the same I will be using in this book, it will be easier for you to use the same program I do.

To get *Brackets* go to

brackets.io and download the application. Then go through the installation process.

STEP 2

Once your program is installed, create a folder in which you will save all your website files. For example, save them on your desktop with a folder called "My First Site".

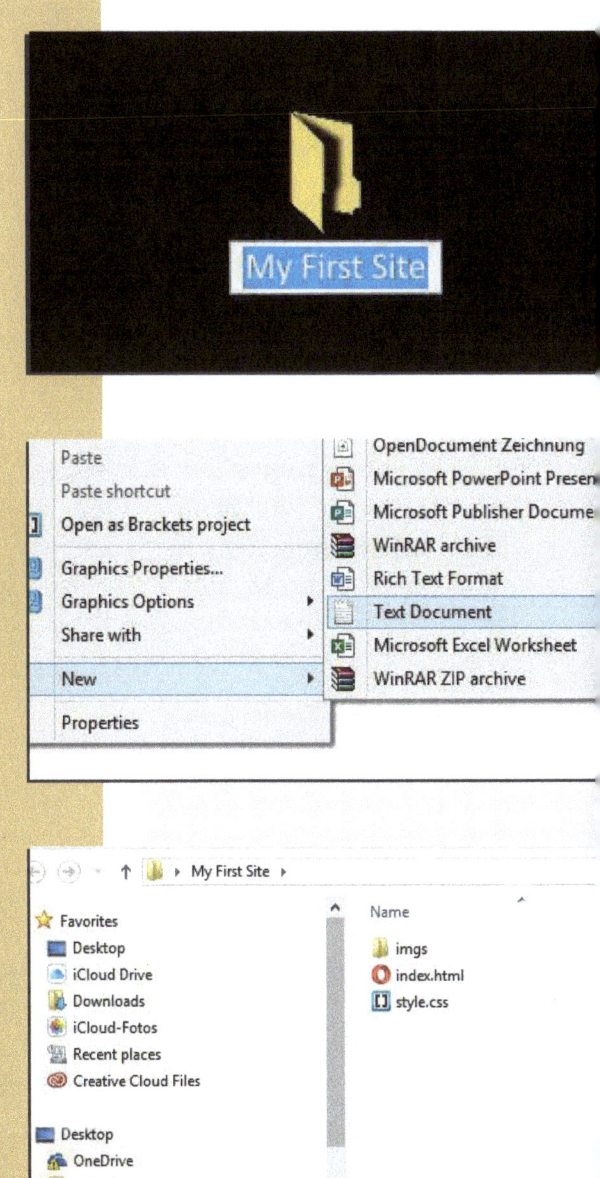

After that, create an "index.html" file. "Index" is the file, your browser is looking for when it opens your website. It is necessary to name the file this way in order to work properly. To do this simply right click in your opened "My First Site" folder, create a text file and change the extension from ".txt" to ".html".

Create a "style.css"

file and an images folder. You will use the style file later on to customize your website with the programming language *CSS*. The images folder is simply a place where you can save all the images you will use. Call it "imgs".

STEP 3

Step 3 is required if you use *Brackets*. Install a tool called *beautify*. It turns messy code into clean code.

In case you don't use *Brackets* you can use the online tool: "https://beautifier.io".

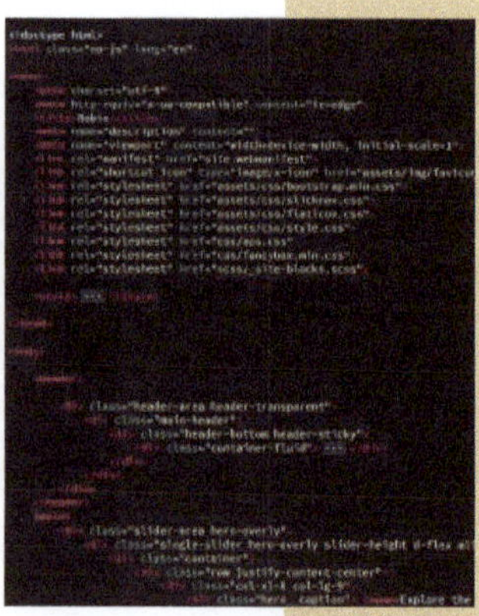

1. Open *Brackets* and click on File > Extension Manager
2. Enter "*beautify*" in the search bar and hit on "Install"
3. Reload/reopen *Brackets*

Now every time you want to use the extension "*beautify*" you can either click on Edit > "*beautify*" or use the shortcut "Ctrl + ALT + B" for Windows or for Mac "Shift + Command + L".

You will be amazed at how your code becomes more readable.

 Extra tip:

On your left sidebar, click on the dropdown folder and select the folder you created in step 2. Every time you will open *Brackets* all your website files will open automatically.

HTML BASICS

2.

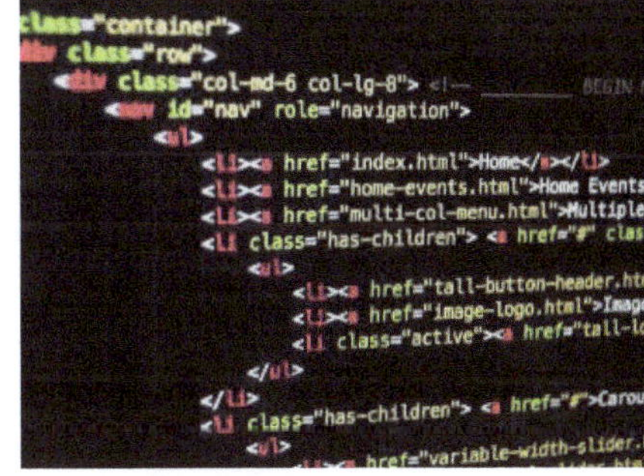

CREATING THE SITE

```
<html>
 <body>
  <h1>Headline</h1>
      <p>You can see a paragraph.
      Write a long text on the subject
      of your choice which is as long
      as you wish.</p>
 </body>
<html>
```

In the example above, you can see some basic *HTML* code. Don't worry about what it means yet. Just notice the red <html></html> *tags* and the black text. This is the way an *HTML* page works.

In *HTML5*, which is the current version, there are over 100 *tags*. Each one of these tells the browser what you want to be shown. We will cover a lot of *tags* in this book, but you don't need to know every single one to build a great website.

Tags are made of an opening "<" and a closing ">" bracket. Usually you also need to close them with a closing *tag*: "</html>".

BASIC STRUCTURE

```
<!Doctype html>
<html>
  <head>
    <title>Robin</title>
  </head>

  <body>

    <!--Your Tags and
    content-->

    <h1>Headline</h1>
    <p>You can see a
    paragraph. Write a long
    text on the subject of
    your choice which is as
    long as you wish.</p>
  </body>
<html>
```

WHAT DOES THIS MEAN?

<!DOCTYPE HTML>

Let's take a closer look at the *doctype*:
It is the first element you will see on a website. It is not really a *tag*. It's just information that tells the browser what kind of document to expect. In *HTML5* you can simply write:

```
<!doctype html>
```

In older versions of *HTML* the *doctype* used to look like this:

```
<!DOCTYPE HTML PUBLIC "-//W3C//DTD HTML 4.01 Transitional//EN" "http:// www.w3.org /TR/html4/loose.dtd">
```

<HTML>

The first *tag* in the *HTML* document is the <html> *tag*. It represents the root of the document and tells the browser that it actually is an *HTML* document.

It is the *container* of all the other elements on the page, except for the <!doctype html> which comes first.

The <html> *tag* has basically two *children*. In other words, all the *tags* on your document are 'subtags' inside of the <html> *tag*.

<HEAD>

Remember: everything that goes inside of your <head> *tag* will not be visible on the actual webpage.

Metaphorically speaking, it is the brain of the webpage.

WHAT TAGS ARE USED IN THE HEAD TAG ?

The *head* can include the following *tags*:

- <title>

- <style>
- <base>
- <link>
- <meta>
- <script>
- <noscript>

HEAD TAGS EXPLAINED

The **<title>** *tag* is necessary in every web-page.

Your browser will display the title on the *tab* of your site. Simply type in the name you want to appear on the *tab* of your browser.

The **<style>** *tags* are used for *CSS*. You can either include your *CSS* code directly inside of the tags like in the picture on the right, or you can link an external ".css" file.

We will link an external ".css" file to make your code cleaner.

```
<link rel="stylesheet" href="scss/_site-blocks.scss">

<style>
    .col-12 {
        padding: 0
    }

    .align-items-stretch {
        margin: 0
    }

    .col-6 {
        padding: 0
    }

    .img-fluid {
        width: 100%;
        object-fit: cover;
        height: 300px;
        margin-bottom: 5px;
        vertical-align: middle;
        -webkit-box-sizing: border-box;
```

The **<base>** *tag* transforms every link on the page with the *value* you give it.

For example if you write:
<base href="https://www.robinbr.com/">

Every link you add, will now direct the user to "robinkbr.com/yourlink".

With the **<link>** *tag* you can link or 'connect' your current 'index.html' document to another external resource like a 'style.css' document.

To link a file, simply type the following code in the *head* of your 'index.html':

```
<link rel="stylesheet"
href="style.css">
```

The 'rel' *attribute* simply indicates the relationship between the current document and the linked document.

On the example above the linked document is a stylesheet (a '*CSS* file'). You can also link an icon or a license.

The <link> *tag* also allows you to add your *favicon*. It is the small website icon you see in every browser *tab*.

"Png" and "ico" are image extensions. You can use the one or the other as long as the image has the right size.

Go to "[www.favicon-generator.org]()" and create your *favicon* easily.

Import your own image or use one of the images from the gallery of the site. Once you click on "Create Favicon", you will get a ".zip" file. Extract it.

You will get several images in different sizes. The browser will automatically use the small images when the user has a slow internet connection and the large images when the user's connection is faster. It is recommended to have at least 3 sizes on your website.

Recommended Sizes:

- 32x32
- 96x96
- 192x192

Repeat the following code for every *favicon* size you want to implement. Pay attention to save your images in the right folder and to link them properly.

```
<link rel="icon"
type="image/png"
sizes="192x192"
 href="yourfolder/and
roid-icon-
192x192.png">
```

The next *tag* is **<meta>**. It provides *metadata* about the *HTML* document. You will not be able to see it on your page, but search engines like Google, Bing or Yahoo can use it to rank your site higher or lower on their platforms.

You can add the following details:

- Keywords
- Author
- Description
- Viewport

To add these *tags*, use the following code:

```
<meta name="keywords" content="HTML,CSS,JavaScript, learn webdesign, create a website">

<meta name="author" content="Robin">

<meta name="description" content="Create your Website">
```

The *viewport metadata* is extremely important, especially for mobile devices. In the past when websites were only available on desktops, you had the same *viewport* for your PC and your mobile device. As a result websites looked horrible on your phone and browsers were forced to scale the screen until the user could see the text and the links.

In the pictures above, you can see the difference between a set and an unset *viewport*.

Use this line to include the *viewport*:

```
<meta name="viewport"
content="width=device
-width, initial-
scale=1">
```

Additionally, you can use the <meta> *tag* to allow special characters like "ä, ö, ü, é, ©".

Include the following line on the <head> of your website:

```
<meta charset="UTF-
8">
```

The next *tag* is **<script>**. It is used to include the programming language *JavaScript* in your document. *JavaScript* is one of the three web programming languages and this book covers some basics.

You can either write your *JavaScript* code directly inside the *tag* or in an external file:

```
<script>
  document.write("
  Hello World!")
</script>
```

Link it to an external 'script.js 'file with the following line:

```
<script
src="script.js" >
</script>
```

Notice *JavaScript* might also be embedded at the bottom of your <body>. The browser will then load all your elements first and apply the script afterwards.

The last <head> *tag* is **<noscript>**. It defines an alternative content for users that either disabled *JavaScript* in their browser or have a browser that does not support *JavaScript*. Nowadays every new browser supports this language.

To add <noscript> use this line:

```
<noscript>
  Your browser does
  not support
  JavaScript.
</noscript>
```

ACTION STEPS

Open your 'index.html' file and use the information you have just learned:

Add the following *tags* in the right order:

- <html></html>
- <body></body>
- <head></head>
- <!doctype html>

In your *head* apply the following points:

1. Allow your website to use special characters such as "ä, ö, ü, é, ©".
2. Add a title to your site.
3. Add a description, and keywords with the <meta> *tag*.
4. Set your *viewport*.
5. Link a *favicon*.
6. Link your 'style.css' file.

It is important that you implement what you have learned in order to retain as much information as possible. Do not continue reading until this step is completed.

YOUR CODE:

```
<!doctype html>
<html>

<head>

  <meta charset="utf-8">

  <title>Robin</title>

  <meta name="description" content="HTML &
  CSS">
  <meta name="author" content="Robin">
  <meta name="description" content="HTML
  Book">

  <meta name="viewport"
  content="width=device-width,initial-
  scale=1">

  <link rel="shortcut icon" type="image/png"
  href="imgs/favicon_192x192.png">

  <link rel="stylesheet" href="style.css">

</head>

<body>

</body>

</html>
```

BODY TAGS EXPLAINED

<BODY>

Let's take a closer look on the <body>. This *tag* defines everything you will see on the actual page.

Example:

```
<body>
  <h1>My Headline</h1>
  <p>My long paragraph. Write a
  long text about any subject.
  </p>
</body>
```

My Headline

My long paragraph. Write a long text about any subject.

I recommend you to experiment with the code as you keep reading. This way you, you will learn faster and it will be easier for you to create your site.

Throughout the following pages, you are going to learn some *tags* that can directly be added in the <body> of your 'index.html' file.

<H1>

<h1> is a *tag* used to display headlines. You might also use <h2>, <h3>, <h4>, <h5> and <h6>.

The <h2> heading will be displayed smaller than the <h1> but larger than the <h3> headline.

Heading 1

Heading 2

Heading 3

Heading 4

Heading 5

Heading 6

<P>

The <p> *tag* defines a paragraph. You should use it to write longer text passages such as descriptions or blog posts.

Lorem Ipsum is simply dummy text of the printing and typesetting industry. Lorem Ipsum has been the industry's standard dummy text ever since the 1500s, when an unknown printer took a galley of type and scrambled it to make a type specimen book. It has survived not only five centuries, but also the leap into electronic typesetting, remaining essentially unchanged. It was popularised in the 1960s with the release of Letraset sheets containing Lorem Ipsum passages, and more recently with desktop publishing software like Aldus PageMaker including versions of Lorem Ipsum.

<B>

<b> stands for bold and does exactly what it sounds like. It shows your text in bold.

Example: Text

```
<p>My paragraph includes <b> important text </b>. </p>
```

My paragraph includes **important text**

<I>

The <i> *tag* shows your text in italic.

Example: Text

```
<p> My paragraph includes <i> italic text </i>. </p>
```

My paragraph includes *italic text*

<U>

With the <u> *tag* you can underline your text.

Yet it is not recommen-ded to use it since it can easily be confused with a link.

Example: Text

```
<p>My paragraph includes <u> under
```

```
lined text </u>. </p>
```

My paragraph includes <u>underlined text </u>.

<STRIKE>

With the <strike> *tag* you can cross text passages.

Example: Text

```
<p>My paragraph
includes <strike>
unimportant text
</strike>. </p>
```

My paragraph includes ~~unimportant text~~.

 adds a line break. It is an empty *tag* which means that it has no end *tag*.

```
<p> My paragraph incl
udes <br> a break and
<br><br> a second
break </p>
```

My paragraph includes
a break and

a second break

<DIV>

<div> is one of the most important *tags*. It stands for division and is a *container* for other *tags*. It is mainly used to either style itself or its *children elements* with *CSS*, or to perform certain *JavaScript* actions.

```
<div>
  <p>My paragraph
  here</p>
</div>
```

You will only see a difference in your browser, if you add some styling.

```
<div style="color:
cadetblue">
  <p>My paragraph
```

My paragraph here

<A>

With the <a> *tag* you can add links to either an external site such as 'google.com' or to another page on your site.

For example on the site 'robinkbr.com' you can click on 'portfolio'. It will bring you to 'robinkbr .com/portfolio'. It is still the same website, but a different webpage.

External Page:

```
<a href="https://www.google.com">Google</a>
```

Same Page:

```
<a href="portfolio/index.html">Google</a>
```

Google

<IMG>

Using this *tag* you can link an image to your website.

Use one of your images, paste it into your images folder and add the following line:

```
<img src="imgs/youriamge.jpg" alt="Your image name">
```

The 'alt' *attribute* is necessary for search-engines to find your content.

Its width will depend on the actual image size.

Change the size with a width *attribute*:

```
<img src="img/yourimage.jpg" alt="Your image name" width="300px">
```

If you want to use an image as a link, add the <a> *tag* around your image:

```
<a
href="https://google
.com">
  <img
  src="imgs/cat.png"
  alt="Cat"
  width="300px">
</a>
```

If you don't want the image to adjust its width and height, use the *CSS attribute* "*object-fit*".

ADDITIONAL USEFUL TAGS

<VIDEO>

The video *tag* allows you to embed an offline video. Supported are '.mp4', '.ogg' and '.WebM' documents.

```
<video controls>
  <source
  src="video.mp4"
  type="video/mp4">
  <source
  src="video.ogg"
  type="video/ogg">
  Your browser does
  not support the
  video tag.
</video>
```

In the **src** *attribute* write the location where the video is stored.

The **controls** *attribute* adds buttons like play, pause and a time bar.

You can also add an **autoplay** *attribute* which

will start the video as soon as it has finished loading.

The **poster** *attribute* links an image as a preloader as long as the video has not been loaded:

```
<video autoplay controls poster="imgs/google.png">
  <source src="video.mp4" type="video/mp4">
  <source src="video.ogg" type="video/ogg">
  Your browser does not support the video tag.
</video>
```

In case you want to start the video at a specific time you can add '#t={**starttime**},{**endtime**}' at the end of your source:

```
<video autoplay controls poster="imgs/google.png">
  <source src="video.mp4#t=10,20" type="video/mp4">
  <source src="video.ogg#t=10,20" type="video/ogg">
  Your browser does not support the video tag.
</video>
```

<IFRAME>

<iframe> is used to embed other documents in your webpage. For example, you could embed a YouTube video:

```
<iframe src="https://www.youtube.com/embed/yourvideo" allow="autoplay; encrypted-media;" frameborder="0" allowfullscreen></iframe>
```

By adding "**?autoplay=1**" at the end of the source, your video will start automatically.

Adding "**&loop=1**" will play the video again once it is finished.

Using "**?controls=0**" will remove the controls from

your video.

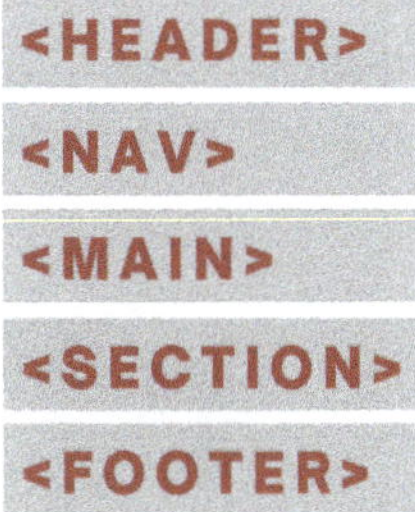

The five *tags* above simply allow the coder to clarify his/her code. The *tags* have the same characteristics as a division, but they are used in different places in the code.

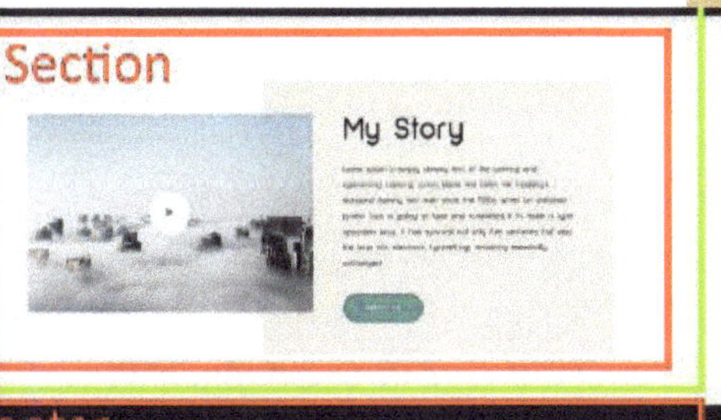

The **<header>** will be the first element you add in your *body*. As you can see in the picture on the previous page it is the overall *container* of the top navigation bar. It contains either a headline such as <h1>, <h2>, <h3>, ... or a logo.

The **<nav>** *tag* stands for navigation. It is often a *child* of the <header> and the *container* of all the links on the top naviga-tion bar, except for the logo and headlines.

<main> is the *container* of every section on your site.

The sections are a clean way to define where your content begins and where it ends. On the picture in the last page you can see a section with a video preview and description on its right. Another example of a section might be a slideshow, a testimonial, an advertising banner or a blog preview.

The last *tag* is the **<footer>**. This *tag* is

included on every page and is the *container* of the bottom links and statements like "Copy-right all rights reserved".

<SPAN>

The span *tag* is used to group inline elements.

Example:

```
<p>My text is long and complicated and this <span color="cadetblue"> word <span>
is especially important</p>
```

Just for the purpose of changing the color of a word you wouldn't create a new division. In general spans are used for single words that need slight adjustments.

<UL>

<LI>

The <ul> and <li> *tags*, create unordered lists. You will see them in the top navigation of a website and on general lists.

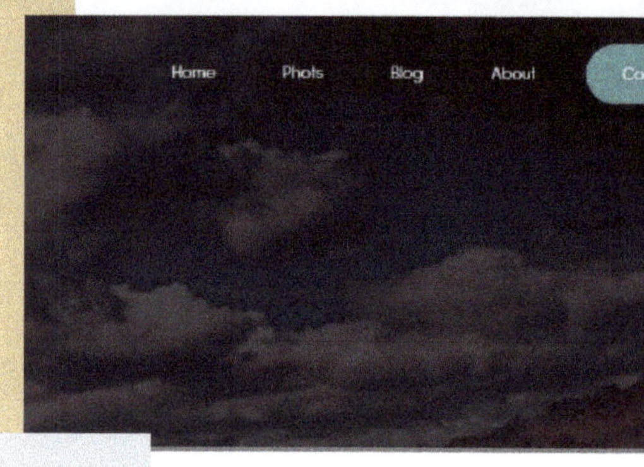

- Element 1
- Element 2
- Element 3
- Element 4

```
<ul>
  <li>Element 1</li>
  <li>Element 2</li>
<ul>
```

<HR>

This *tag* is used as a line between two elements.

ease of Letraset sheets containing Lorem Ipsum ssages, and more recently with desktop publishing ftware like Aldus PageMaker including versions of rem Ipsum.

---

rem Ipsum is simply dummy text of the printing d typesetting industry. Lorem Ipsum has been the lustry's standard dummy text ever since the 1500s, ıen an unknown printer took a galley of type and ambled it to make a type specimen book. It has rvived not only five centuries, but also the leap into ctronic typesetting, remaining essentially changed. It was popularised in the 1960s with the ease of Letraset sheets containing Lorem Ipsum ssages, and more recently with desktop publishing

<!--COMMENT-->

The comments will not be used by your browser in any way. They only allow the coders to keep their code clean and write notes in-between two elements.

```
<br>
<!--This tag displays a line-->

<p>Lorem Ipsum is simply dummy text of t
typesetting industry. Lorem Ipsum has be
industry's standard dummy text ever sinc
```

<FORM>

This *tag* is used to create an *HTML* form.

In the most common ones, the user can submit his/her Firstname, Last-name and email address.

These are the most common *tags* used in combination with a form:

- label
- input
- textarea
- select
- option
- button

Usual structure of a form:

```
<form
action="process.php">
  <label
for="name">Name:
</label>
  <input type="text"
id="name"
name="name"><br><br>
  <label
for="email">Email:
</label>
  <input type="text"
id="email"
name="email"><br><br>
```

```
<input type="submit"
value="Submit">
</form>
```

Name:

Email:

Submit

<INPUT>

The input field specifies an area in which the user can enter his/her information. He/she can enter anything from name and e-mail to phone number and the product being purchased.

The code of an <input> *tag*:

```
<input type="text"
id= "email"
name="email">
```

<LABEL>

This *tag* allows you to add a label to a specific input field.

```
<label
for="email">Email:
</label>
```

<SELECT>

<OPTION>

The <select> and <option> *tags* are used to create dropdown menus.

Option 1

This is the usual structure of the select and option *tags*:

```
<select
id="dropdown">
  <option
  value="optn1">Opti
  on 1</option>
  <option
  value="optn2">Opti
  on 2</option>
  <option
  value="optn3">Opti
  on 3</option>
  <option
  value="optn4">Opti
  on 4</option>
</select>
```

<TEXTAREA>

You might want to add an extra field for comments or special favors at the end of your form.

This *tag* comes at the end of a form and uses the following code:

```
<textarea
id="textarea"
rows="5" cols="50">
My textarea
</textarea>
```

The 'row' *attribute* specifies the height of your textarea. The 'cols' *attribute* its width.

<BUTTON>

This *tag* creates a clickable button. You can add either text to it or an image.

Note that the default buttons look like the image below, but if you want to edit them, you must use *CSS*.

ACTION STEPS

Open your 'index.html' file and use what you have just learned.

In the *body* of your document, add the following *tags* in the right order:

- <nav>
- <header>
- <main>
- <footer>
- <section>

Within the <section> create three paragraphs with text and use two words as a link to an external website.

- At least one word or passage is shown in bold.
- At least one image must be added.

YOUR CODE:

```
...
<body>

  <header>
    <nav></nav>
  </header>


  <main>
    <section>

      <p>Lorem ipsum is a dummy <a
      href="https://www.robinkbr.com">
      <b>Robin</b></a>.</p>

      <p>Lorem ipsum is a dummy <a
      href="https://www.robinkbr.com">Google
      </a>.</p>

      <p>Lorem ipsum is a dummy text.</p>

      <img src="imgs/cat.png">

    </section>
  </main>

  <footer></footer>

</body>
```

CSS BASICS

3.

ATTRIBUTES

```
<p class="red-p"
id="paragraph1">
</p>
```

You might have noticed that *HTML tags* are composed of *attributes*. For example the <a> *tag* uses the *attribute* "href=" to link the website you want to include on your site:
<a href="https://www.google.com"></a>

The *tags* you add to your site such as <div>, <p>, <a>, <span>, <h1> also use what is called *classes* and *ids*. An *id* is unique to an *element* and can only be used by one specific *tag* on the page. A *class* on the other hand can be used by multiple elements at the same time.

These *attributes* are used by *CSS* documents to find the *tags* and sections you want to customize.

EXAMPLE


```
<!Doctype html>
<html>
  <head>
    <style>
      p {
        font-family: cursive;
       }
      .red-p {
        color: red;
      }
      #paragraph1 {
        font-size: 25px;
      }
    </style>
  </head>

  <body>

    <p>Text</p>
    <p class="red-p">Text</p>
    <p class="red-p"
    id="paragraph1">Text </p>

  </body>
<html>
```

WHAT IS CSS ?

```
p {color: red;}
```

CSS stands for *Cascading Style Sheets*. It describes how *HTML* elements are displayed on the screen and it can completely change the way a document looks like.

A simple example is the code on the previous page. If the style did not say "color: red" and "font size: 20px" but "color: green" and "font size: 200px". It would not look the same.

This is a simple example, but it does also apply for bigger code passages. Remember: the style defines how a website looks like.

Do not include the *CSS* code directly in the *HTML* document. Earlier in this book under "getting started" > "step 2" you created a document called "style.css". This is the document you will put all the *CSS* code in. Remember to **link** it in the *head* of of your *HTML* document.

HOW CSS WORKS

A *CSS rule-set* consists of a *selector* and a *declaration*. The *declaration* is divided into a *property* and a *value*:

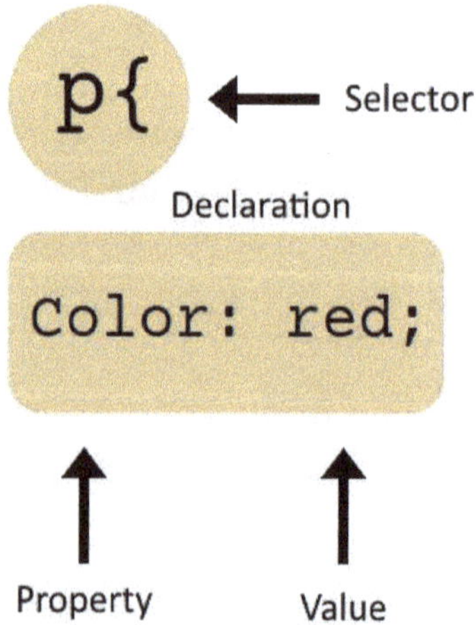

The semicolon at the end of each *declaration* is necessary. If you forget it, the next *declaration* will not work. Fortunately, if you forget it, your *HTML* editor will show it by changing the color of the next line.

Example of some *CSS* code:

```
p {
color: black;
text-align: center;
font-size: 20px;
font-family: serif;
}

.red-p {
color: red;
}
```

Note: basic *tags* are referred to by their *tagname*. For example, you can change the style of every paragraph on your site by using the name "*p*".

```
p {
   color:red;
}
```

In this case the text of every paragraph will be red.

Classes are referred to by a ".":

```
.red-p {
   color:red;
}
```

And *ids* are referred to by a "#":

```
#paragraph1{
   color:red;
}
```

CSS can be added in 3 different ways:

- With an external document (what you should do)
- With a style *attribute* inside the *head* of a document (page 43)
- As an *attribute* to your *tag* like in the example underneath:

```
<p style="color:red; font-size: 20px"></p>
```

BASIC DECLA-RATIONS

COLOR:

The color *property* refers to the color of a text:

```
color: purple;

color: red;
```

A color can also be specified by its "color code" like RGB, HEX, HSL, RGBA and HSLA:

RGBA & HSL/HSLA colors were introduced in *CSS3*. Until *CSS2* only RGB colors (Red, Green, Blue) were used. RGB and RGBA are screen colors and not recommended for printing. The total number of colors in RGB amounts to 16 million. But *CSS3* also supports RGBA, HSL and HSLA colors. HSL stands for Hue, Saturation, Lightness.

RGB colors are declared in RGB or hexadecimal format. For example, the color black is written as red, rgb(0, 0, 0), #000000 and #000. RGBA colors are the same as RGB colors, but they have an additional fourth *value*: Alpha. Alpha is the degree of opacity of the color. Therefore, solid red color can also be written as rgba(0, 0, 0, 1).

FONT:

The font *property* allows you to edit the font of your text.

It can be broken down into 4 categories.

FONT-FAMILY:

FONT-STYLE:

FONT-WEIGHT:

FONT-SIZE:

With the **font-family** you can change the type of font you use (Arial, Calibri, Times New Roman):

```
p {
  font-family: "Times
  New Roman", sans -
  serif.
}
```

The comma after "Times New Roman" means if this font cannot be loaded, it automatically uses one of the 5 basic *HTML* fonts included in every browser:

- cursive
- fantasy
- monospace
- sans-serif
- serif

At one point or another you might see this *declaration*:

```
font-family: inherit;
```

It simply means that the element uses the same *value* as its *parent* element.

Note that you can use this *value* for every *CSS property* not only "font".

Font-style:
The font weight *declaration* is mostly used for italic text.

```
.red-p {
  font-style: italic;
}
```

Font-weight:
This *declaration* is used to define the boldness of your text.

```
p {
  font-weight: bold;
}

div {
  font-weight:
  bolder;
}

.bold-p {
  font-weight: 700;
}
```

You can either use the *values* "bold" and "bolder" or you can use numbers between 100 and 1000 for a more accurate estimation.

Font-size:
Use this *property* to define the size of your text:

```
p {
  font-size: 20px;
}
```

The overall *property* **"font"** combines all the *properties* above.

It is used in this order:
style - weight - size - family

```
font: italic, bold,
20px, sans-serif;
```

BACKGROUND:

You can use this *property* in several circumstances:

BACKGROUND-

- **COLOR:**
- **IMAGE:**
- **POSITION:**
- **ATTACHMENT:**
- **SIZE:**

The **background-color** *property* specifies the background color of an element.

```
div, p {
  background-color:
  red;
}
```

My Paragraph

The **background-image** defines the image of an element.

```
div {
  background-image:
  url("https://fr.wik
  ipedia.org/wiki/Fic
  hier:Google.png");
}

.myimg {
  background-image:
  url("imgs/google.pn
  g");
}
```

Note that in order to see the image, you need to add the *properties* "width" and "height", which we will discuss on the next page.

Background-position defines the position of your image.

```
div {
  background-
  position: top left;
}
div {
  background-
  position: center;
}
```

You can add *values* such as: 'top', 'right', 'bottom', 'left', but in most cases it is a good idea to have it centered because you can see the middle parts of an image.

The **background-attachment** defines how the image scrolls. You can set it to: "scroll" or "fixed". Scroll is the default *value* and you will not see any changes on the scroll behavior of your image. If you set it to fixed though the image will not scroll with the page. It will simply stay at the same place and will get covered with your page elements and sections.

```
div {
  background-
  attachment: scroll;
}
div {
```

```
  background-
  attachment: fixed;
}
```

The **background-size** *property* sets the scale of your image. You can set it to a specific percentage like "100%". The width of your image will then be set to 100% of its *container*. You can also set it to "100% 50%". This *value* will set the width to "100%" and the height to "50%".

Most of the time you should use the *declaration* "background-size: cover". The image will then cover the entire *container* even if it has to cut some parts off.

If the "background-size" is set to "contain", the image will not cover the entire *container*, but it will be entirely visible.

Background-size: cover

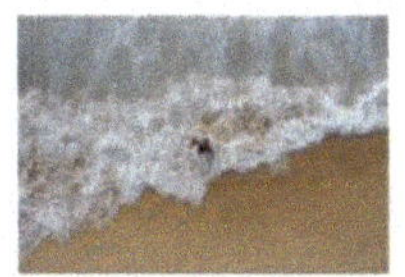

Background-size: contain

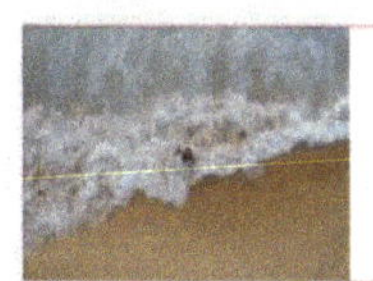

You can also combine all these *properties* into one:

```
background: red
url("imgs/google.png")
cover no-repeat
center;
```

The right order is:

1. Color
2. Url
3. Size
4. Repeat
5. Position

WIDTH: & HEIGHT:

If you try to create a division and you add a background image, it will not work. This is simply because the default width and height *values* for this subdivision are "0".

To change these *properties* simply add a *value* in "px" or in "%" of its *container*.

```
div {
   width: 600px;
   height: 400px;
}

.myimage {
   width: 100%;
   height: 500px;
}
```

You can also calculate a certain width in combination with a px *value*:

```
.myimage {
   width: calc(100% -
   100px);
   height: 300px;
   background: red;
}
```

If you want to use the width or the height of your screen, use the unit "vh" for the height and "vw" for the width.

```
.myimage {
   width: calc(100% -
   100px);
   height: 300px;
   background: red;
}
```

ACTION STEPS

1. Remove the paragraphs and the images inside the section of your *body*.
2. In the same section create a *division* and add a class to it.
3. In your 'style.css' file add this element and give it a "width" of "100%" and a "height" of "100vh".
4. Download a wallpaper from the internet and add it to your images folder.
5. Then add a "background-image" and disable "background-repeat".
6. Set the "background-position" to "top left" and experiment with the size.

YOUR HTML CODE:

```
...
<body>

  <header>
    <nav></nav>
  </header>


  <main>

    <section>
      <div class="myimage"></div>
    </section>

  </main>

  <footer></footer>

</body>
```

YOUR CSS CODE:

```
.myimage {
  width: 100%;
  height: 100vh;
  background-color: red;
  background-image: url(imgs/wallpaper.jpg);
  background-repeat: no-repeat;
  background-position: top left;
  background-size: contain;
}
```

ADDITIONAL CSS PROPERTIES

THE BOX MODEL

The *CSS* box model is a box that wraps around each *HTML* element. It consists of: margin, border, padding and content.

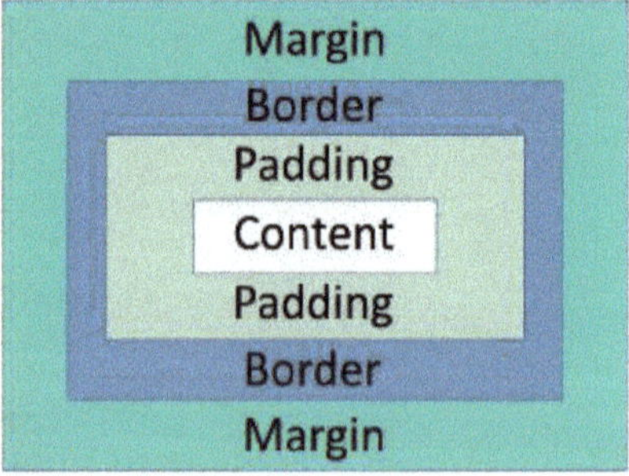

Explanation:

In the *content* you define the width, height and background image of your element. In the first image to the right, the *content* is simply the text of the button.

The **PADDING:** defines the space around the *content* and within defined borders.

You can also change the top, right, bottom, or left *padding* individually with the following *properties*:

- padding-top
- padding-right
- padding-bottom
- padding-left

In the example above the *padding* is set to "10px" on the top and bottom and "20px" on the left and right.

These lines show how the *padding* is usually set:

```
padding: 10px 20px;
padding: 10px 20px 10px 20px;
```

The first line sets both the top and bottom and the left and right *paddings* to equal *values*:
Top & Bottom = 10px
Left & Right = 20px

The second line sets the top, right, bottom and the left *value*. It works in a clockwise sense.

BORDER:

The border *property* allows you to adjust the border width, color, and style of an element. When you place a padding on content with a border, the actual border is pushed away and the element appears larger.

Text

Text

With **border-width** you can increase or decrease the size of the borders.

```
border-width: 10px;
```

The **border-style** *declaration* defines the type of border you want.

```
border 2px solid black;
```

Solid:

Text

Dotted:

Text

Dashed:

Text

Mixed:

MARGIN:

The margin is used to create space around the defined borders of an element.

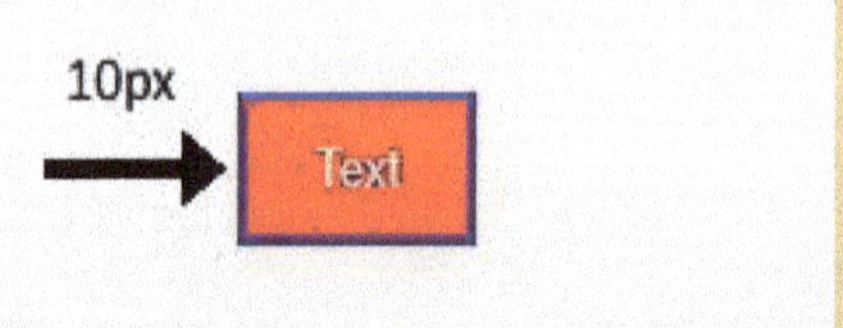

Margins can be set individually:

- `margin-top: 10px;`
- `margin-right: 0;`
- `margin-bottom: 0;`
- `margin-left: 10px;`

You can also set the margin to a specific percentage of its *container*.

```
margin: 10%;
```

The "margin: auto" *property* will center your element horizontally within its *container* as long as you have set the width.

```
<div>
  <p id="p1">Text</p>
</div>
```

```
div {
  width: 50%;
  float: right;
  background: blue;
}

#p1 {
  width: 30px;
  background-color:
  red;
  color: white;
  padding: 20px 10px;
  margin: auto;
}
```

/*COMMENT*/

The comment allows you to keep a clean code by adding your thoughts between the lines.

Comments in *CSS* are written differently than in *HTML*.

/*My Comment is long and goes over several lines*/

BORDER-RADIUS:

You can use the border-radius *property* to create rounded edges on an element:

```
div {
  width: 50px;
  height: 50px;
  background: red;
  border-radius: 10px;
}
```

POSITION:

The position *property* defines the type of positioning of an element. The positioning is set through the top, right, bottom and left *properties*. The most common *values* are listed below:

- static /*default*/
- relative
- absolute
- fixed

Static elements are not affected by top, right, bottom and left *proper-ties.* They are not considered as "position-ed".
Relative positioned elements, will move away from their normal position.

An absolute positioned element is relative to its next positioned *container*. It represents a *container* that is not static. You can move an absolute positioned element along its *container*.

```
.div1 {
  position: relative;
  width: 100%;
  height: 200px;
  background: red;
}

.div2 {
  position: absolute;
  width: 200px;
  height: 200px;
  background: blue;
  left: 20px;
}
```

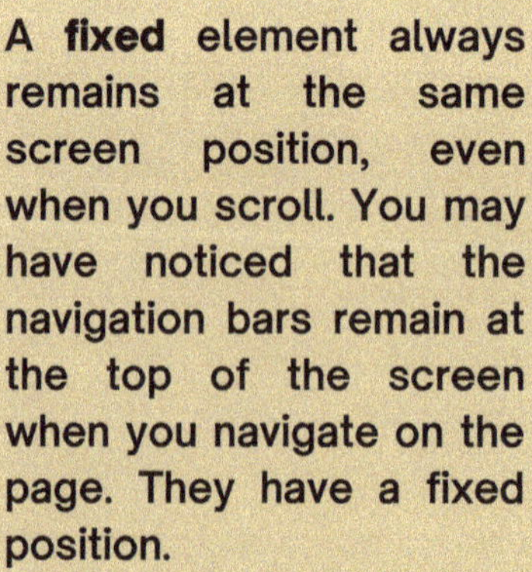

A **fixed** element always remains at the same screen position, even when you scroll. You may have noticed that the navigation bars remain at the top of the screen when you navigate on the page. They have a fixed position.

My Story

Lorem Ipsum is simply dummy text of the printing and typesetting industry. Lorem Ipsum has been the industry's standard dummy text ever since the 1500s, when an unknown printer took a

Z-INDEX:

The z-index *property* allows you to bring an element forward in the stack of elements:

z-index works only on positioned elements.

Notice: elements that are lower in your code will automatically be shown further ahead, without having a greater z-index *value*.

```
.div1 {
  position: absolute;
  width: 200px;
  height: 200px;
  background: red;
  z-index: 3;
}

.div2 {
  position: absolute;
  width: 200px;
  height: 200px;
  background: blue;
  top: 50px;
  left: 50px;
  z-index: 2;
}

.div3 {
  position: absolute;
  width: 200px;
  height: 200px;
  background: green;
  top: 100px;
  left: 100px;
  z-index: 1;
}
```

FLOAT:

The float *property* is used to position and format content. You can float text in a *container* to the left of an image.

For example:

```
div {
  width: 200px;
  height: 200px;
  background: red;
  float: right;
}
```

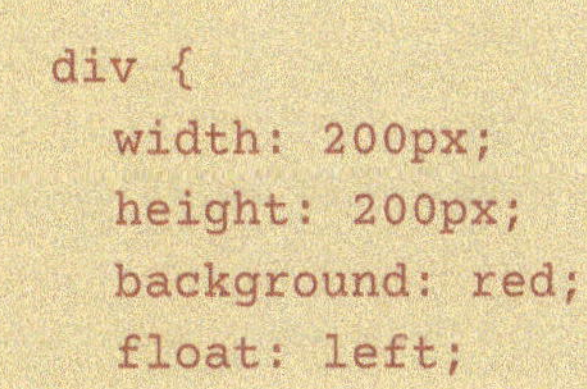

```
div {
  width: 200px;
  height: 200px;
  background: red;
  float: left;
}
```

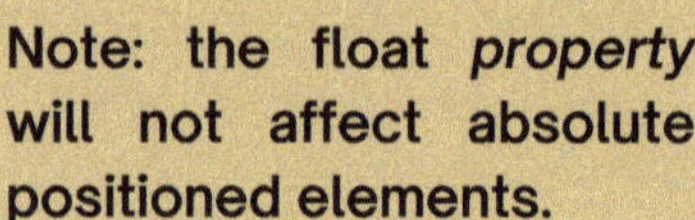

Note: the float *property* will not affect absolute positioned elements.

DISPLAY:

This *property* explains how an element is being displayed on the site. The most important *values* are:

- block
- inline
- inline-block
- none

The display: **block** *declaration* allows an element to take up the entire width of its *container*. It will appear in a new line.

Lorem Ipsum is simply dummy text of the printing and typesetting industry. Lorem Ipsum has been the industry's standard dummy text ever since the 1500s.
Text
Lorem Ipsum is simply dummy text of the printing and typesetting industry.

The display: **inline** *declaration* is the default "display" *value*. The height and width *properties* have no effect.

Lorem Ipsum is simply dummy text of the printin and typesetting industry. Lorem Ipsum has been th industry's standard dummy text ever since the 150 Text Lorem Ipsum is simply dummy text of the printing and typesetting industry.

Display **inline-block** will set your element as an inline element, but you will be able to change the width and the height *property*.

Lorem Ipsum is simply dummy text of the printin and typesetting industry. Lorem Ipsum has been th industry's standard dummy text ever since the 150 Text Lorem Ipsum is simply dummy te of the printing and typesetting industry.

Display **none** will hide your element. The space it takes will also be removed.

VISIBILITY:

The visibility defines whether or not your element is visible. If you set the visibility to hidden it will still take up space on the page, if you set it to "visible" it will appear as it is displayed by default. The most common *values* of the visibility *property* are:

- visible
- hidden

OPACITY:

This *attribute* allows you to set the opacity level of an element.

opacity: 1

opacity: 0.5

opacity: 0.2

ICONS

Icons are not included per default in *CSS*.

To include icons add the following *tag* in the *head* of your 'index.html' file:

```
<script
src="https://kit.font
awesome.com/a076d0539
9.js"></script>
```

The above code allows you to add the Font Awesome toolkit. It is the most popular icon set in the world.

Now add the class of the icon you want to include:

```
<a><i class="fa fa-
play"></i></a>
```

For a reference of all icons visit the following link: https://fontawesome.com/icons

LINKS (PSEUDO-CLASSES)

A *pseudoclass* is used to define a special state of an element. For example, it can be used in the following ways:

1. Style an element when a user moves the mouse over it
2. Visited and unvisited links are designed differently
3. Design an element when it comes into focus

```
a:hover {
  color: red;
}
```

Here are the most common pseudo classes:

```
/* unvisited link */
a:link {
  color: white;
}

/* visited link */
a:visited {
  color: red;
}

/* mouse over link */
a:hover {
  color: blue;
}

/* selected link */
a:active {
  color: green;
}
```

PSEUDO ELEMENTS

The pseudo-elements can be used to edit parts of an element. For example, it can be used to edit the first line, first letter or last letter of an element. The most common ones are:

- ::first-line
- ::first-letter
- ::before
- ::after

"p::first-line" is used to edit the first line of a paragraph:

```
p::first-line {
  color:red;
}
```

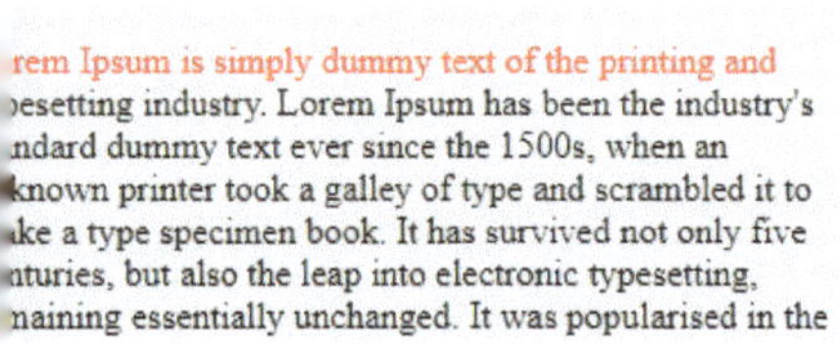

rem Ipsum is simply dummy text of the printing and
›esetting industry. Lorem Ipsum has been the industry's
ndard dummy text ever since the 1500s, when an
known printer took a galley of type and scrambled it to
ke a type specimen book. It has survived not only five
nturies, but also the leap into electronic typesetting,
naining essentially unchanged. It was popularised in the

With "p::first-letter" you can edit the first letter of a text:

```
p::first-letter{
  color:red;
  font-size: 30px;
}
```

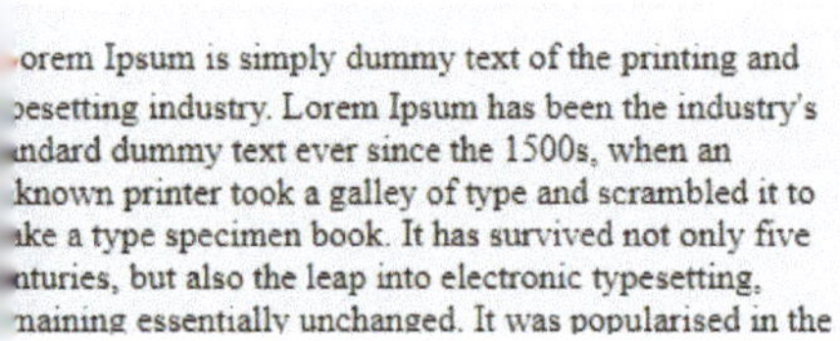

orem Ipsum is simply dummy text of the printing and
›esetting industry. Lorem Ipsum has been the industry's
ndard dummy text ever since the 1500s, when an
known printer took a galley of type and scrambled it to
ke a type specimen book. It has survived not only five
nturies, but also the leap into electronic typesetting,
naining essentially unchanged. It was popularised in the

"div:: before" adds content before the element you target:

```
div::beofre {
  content: "before";
}
```

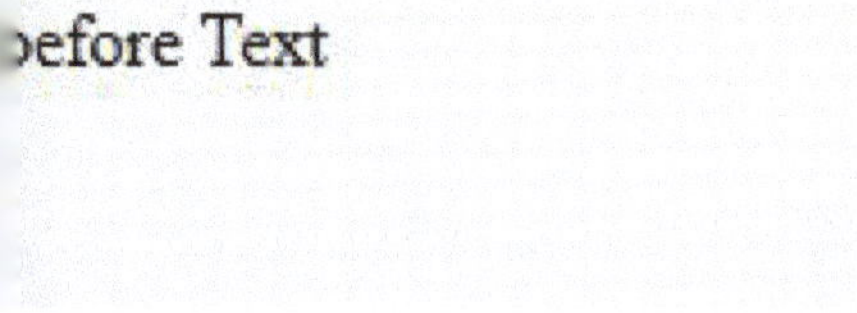

›efore Text

"div::after" adds content before the element you target:

```
div::after{
  content: " after";
}
```

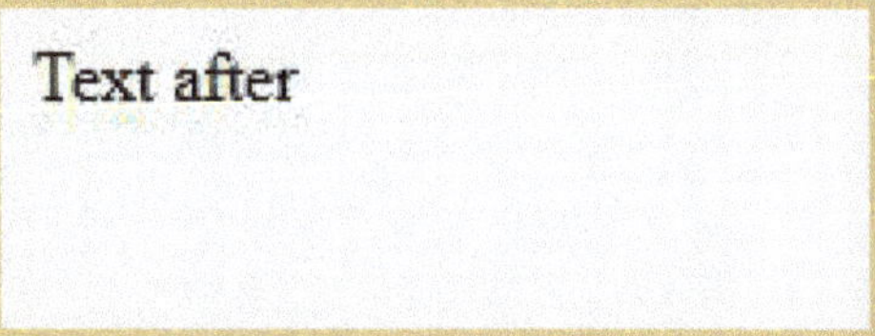

Text after

VARIABLES

Variables are used to save time. You will define a *variable* once and use it throughout your code. You may use it for the main color of your site.

```
:root {
  --main-color: red;
}

.div1 {
  color: var(--main-
  color);
}

p {
  color: var(--main-
  color);
}
```

ANIMATIONS

Animations allow to add movement to your site. To use them, you must define the *keyframes*.

Note: You have to copy your *keyframe* code and add the "@-webkit-" line on your second *keyframe* to make it readable for any browser.

```
@-webkit-keyframes
load {
0% {
   transform:
   rotate(0deg);
}

100% {
   transform:
   rotate(360deg);
}
}

keyframes load {
0% {
   transform:
   rotate(0deg);
}

100% {
   transform:
   rotate(360deg);
}
}

.preloader-cirlce {
   width: 100px;
   height: 100px;
   border-style:
   solid;
   border-width: 1px;
   border-color: red
   transparent
   transparent;
   border-radius: 50%;
   background-color:
   #fff;
   animation:      load
   2000ms     infinite
   ease;
   position: absolute;
   left: 0;
   right: 0;
   top: 0;
   bottom: 0;
   margin: auto;
}
```

Add the Animation *property* to your *CSS* and specify the name of the *keyframes.* In this example it is "load". Then add the time it takes to finish its animation and specify how long it should play.

Also add what is called an animation iteration count. In the example on the previous page it is set to "infinite". (By default it is set to "none").

Finally, you need to define what type of animation you want it to play. The most common animations are:

- ease
- ease-out
- ease-in

The ease *value* specifies an animation effect with a slow start, a faster middle and a slow end (this is the default *value*). The ease-out *value* specifies an animation effect with a slow end. The ease-in specifies an animation effect with a slow start.

You might also see animations that use the "cubic-bezier" *value.* These are very specific types of animations that the coder can define himself/herself.

Go to: cubic-bezier.com to create your own.

Inside the *keyframes* code you see a transform *declaration.* We will go in depth on this *property* on the next page.

THE TRANSFORM PROPERTY

The transform *property* applies 2D and 3D transformations on your element.

It allows you to:

- scale
- rotate
- skew
- move your element around (translate)
- set a perspective to your content

With the animation on the previous page you used the **rotate** *value* to create a loading effect.

The rotate *value* can be used in various styles. Here is another example:

```
transform:
rotate(45deg);
```

The **"Skew"** *property* creates a distortion on the X and Y axes, but you can also isolate the effect one one axis with the "skewX" and "skewY" *values.*

```
transform:
skewX(50deg);
```

```
transform:
skewY(50deg);
```

The **scale** *value* allows you to 'zoom' in or out. The default scale of an element is "1". If you set it to "1.1" it will appear 10% bigger than before.

```
transform: scale(1);
```

```
transform: scale(1.2);
```

```
transform: scale(.8);
```

The translate *property* may have the same result as setting a margin. However, if you want to create an animation, you should not use the margin *property*, as this will create a bugging effect.

```
transform:
translate(0px);
```

```
transform:
translate(10px);
```

```
transform:
translate(10px, 20px);
```

MEDIA QUERIES

Media queries are often used to make your website mobile and desktop friendly. Since you set the height, width, and all your *properties* for one screen size, it does not necessarily mean it will look good on another.

```
@media screen and
(max-width: 480px) {
  body { background-
  color: green;
}}
```

The code on the previous page will set the background color of your *body* to green for the devices with a screen width inferior to 480px.

In the next chapter, you will use *media queries* not to change the background color of your site, but to adjust margins and paddings.

FLEXBOXES

Flexboxes are used to create flexible items within a *container*.

To use flexboxes, add the *declaration* "display: flex" to the *parent* element (the *container*).

```
display: flex;
```

There are several 'flex-exclusive' *properties*. These are the ones you are the most likely to use:

- flex-direction
- flex-grow
- justify-content
- align-items

FLEX-DIRECTION:

The flex direction defines the order in which the elements are displayed.

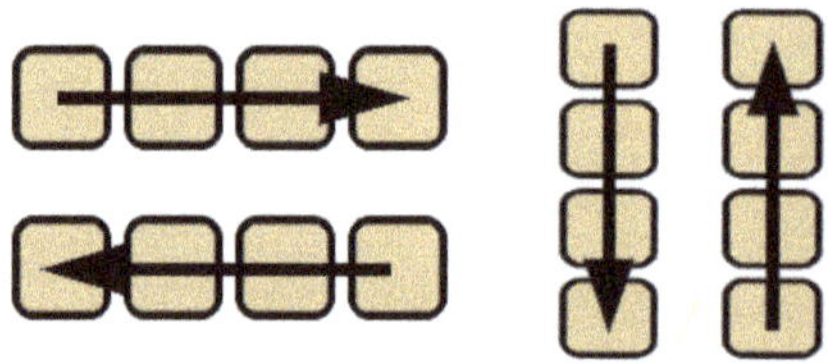

You can change the direction with the following *values*:

- row (default)
- row-reverse
- column
- column-reverse

```
flex-direction: row-reverse;
```

```
flex-direction:
column;
```

```
flex-direction:
column-reverse;
```

FLEX-GROW:

With "flex-grow" you can enlarge one or multiple items within your *container*. It defines how much an element grows in proportion to another.

```
.container div{ flex-
grow: 2; }
```

JUSTIFY-CONTENT:

This *property* allows you to change the way your content is aligned within its *container*. You can set it to:

- flex-start (default)
- flex-end
- center
- space-between
- space-around
- space-evenly

```
.container{  justify-
content: flex-end;}
```

```
.container{  justify-
content: center;}
```

```
.container{ justify-content: space-between;}
```

```
.container{ justify-content: space-around;}
```

```
.container{ justify-content: space-evenly;}
```

ALIGN-ITEMS:

The "align-items" *property* sets the vertical alignment of your items.

```
.container{ align-items: flex-start; }
```

```
.container{ align-items: center; }
```

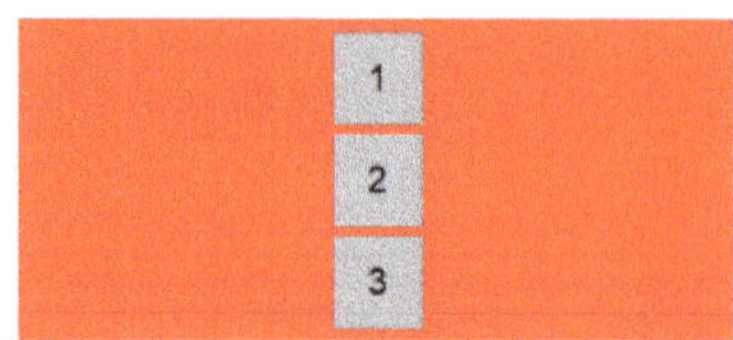


```
.container{ align-items: flex-end; }
```

ACTION STEPS

1. Remove the content in the section of your *body*.
2. Create a subdivision within the main area of your *body* and inside your section area. Give it a *class*.
3. Give it a specific width and height in px and add a background image.
4. Create rounded corners
5. Repeat the four steps once.
6. Make the first image show up further ahead.
7. Use the transform *property* to rotate and scale the second image.

YOUR HTML CODE:

```
...
<body>

  <header>
    <nav></nav>
  </header>


  <main>
    <section>

      <div class="mydiv"></div>
      <div class="mydiv mydiv2"></div>

    </section>
  </main>

  <footer></footer>

</body>
```

YOUR CSS CODE:

```
.mydiv {
  position: absolute;
  width: 200px;
  height: 200px;
  background-image: url(imgs/wallpaper.jpg);
  border-radius: 10px;
  margin: 0;
  z-index: 1;
}

.mydiv2 {
  background-image:
  url(imgs/wallpaper2.jpg);
  margin: 50px;
  z-index: 2;
  transform: rotate(45deg) scale(1.1);
}
```

LIBRARIES & FRAMEWORKS

4.

LIBRARIES & FRAMEWORKS

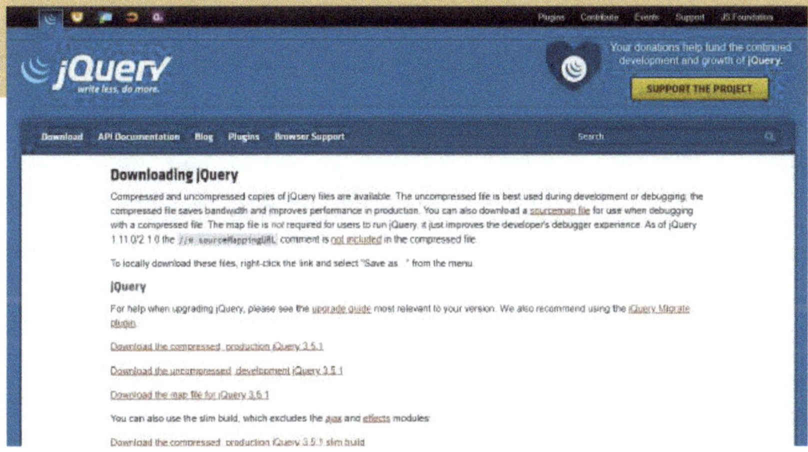

In order to make your site mobile friendly you will not only use *media queries*. You will also use what is called *frameworks*.

A *framework* is a library of pre-modified elements that appears on every website. For example, you will find a navigation bar on each site. The navigation bar will then be styled by the *framework* to look good not only on a desktop computer, but also on a mobile phone.

Notice that *frameworks* are also used to create more complex websites with extra visual features like animations.

Libraries are mainly used by *JavaScript* and are composed of scripts that allow easier development of JavaScript-based applications.

This book covers the following *frameworks* and *libraries*: ***jQuery, Bootstrap, Aos, Fancybox. Slicknav.***

BASICS

JQUERY

jQuery is not really a *framework*. It is a free, open source library designed to simplify *HTML* and *JavaScript* procedures.

It is necessary to include this library in your code in order to continue.

Create a new text document in the folder where you have saved your website documents and name it "jquery". Change the extension to ".js".

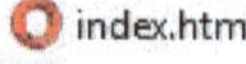
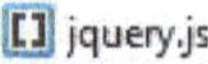

```
imgs
index.html
jquery.js
style.css
```

Now go to jquery.com/download and click on the latest version. A window with the script should open.

```
/*! jQuery v3.5.0 | (c) JS Foundation and other contributors | jquery.org/license
!function(e,t){"use strict";"object"==typeof module&&"object"==typeof module.exp
("undefined"!=typeof window?window:this,function(C,e){"use strict";var t=[],r=Ob
{},o=n.toString,v=n.hasOwnProperty,a=v.toString,l=a.call(Object),y={},m=function
{type:!0,src:!0,nonce:!0,noModule:!0};function b(e,t,n){var r,i,o=(n=n||E).creat
(i=t[r]||t.getAttribute&&t.getAttribute(r))&&o.setAttribute(r,i);n.head.appendCh
f="3.5.0",S=function(e,t){return new S.fn.init(e,t)};function p(e){var t=!!e&&"l
{jquery:f,constructor:S,length:0,toArray:function(){return s.call(this)},get:fun
t.prevObject=this,t},each:function(e){return S.each(this,e)},map:function(n){retu
this.pushStack(s.apply(this,arguments))},first:function(){return this.eq(0)},las
this.pushStack(S.grep(this,function(e,t){return t%2}))},eq:function(e){var t=thi
this.prevObject||this.constructor()},push:u,sort:t.sort,splice:t.splice},S.exten
{},s++),"object"==typeof a||m(a)||(a={}),s===u&&(a=this,s--);s<u;s++)if(null!=(e
[]:i||S.isPlainObject(n)?n:{},i=!1,a[t]=S.extend(l,o,r)):void 0!==r&&(a[t]=r));r
```

Select the entire code by clicking Ctrl + A in windows and Control + A on Mac. Copy and paste the code into the jquery.js file you just created.

Add the following line in your 'index.html' *head tag* to link the "jquery.js" file:

```
<script src="jquery.js"></script>
```

```
    content="HTML,CSS,XML,JavaScript">
    <meta name="author" content="Robin">
    <meta name="description" content="HTML Bo

    <meta name="viewport" content="width=devi
    initial-scale=1.0">

    <link rel="apple-touchicon " sizes="180x1
    gs/apple-touch-icon.png">
    <link rel="icon" type="image/png" sizes="
    href="imgs/favicon-32x32.png">
    <link rel="icon" type="image/png" sizes="
    href="imgs/favicon-16x16.png">
    <link rel="manifest" href="/site.webmanif

    <link rel="stylesheet" href="style.css">


    <script src="js/jquery.js"></script>

</head>
```

BOOTSTRAP

Bootstrap is an open source *framework* that allows you to create mobile first websites. To make a particular element responsive, you will need to add the right classes.

First, you need to add *Bootstrap* to your website. To do this, go to getbootstrap.com and download the latest version.

Unzip the package and add it to your folder.

bootstrap-4.4.1-dist
imgs
index.html
jquery.js
style.css

Now include the *CSS* file in the *head* of your 'index.html' and the script at the bottom of your *body*.

```
<link
rel="stylesheet"
href="bootstrap-
4.4.1-
dist/css/bootstrap.cs
s">
```

```
<script
src="bootstrap-4.4.1-
dist/js/bootstrap.js"
></script>
```

Note: The script *tags* of *plugins* must be added to the bottom of your *body*. Do not add your script *tags* in the *header*, rather add them after the last *tag* of your *body*. The script will then be applied after loading your content.

The following is a short list of classes that you are most likely to use for your websites. In the next chapter you will see many of these classes in action.

CONTAINERS

.CONTAINER

This class limits the width of the current element and sets equal margins on the left and on the right. It will be the *container* of the other *bootstrap* elements for that section.

.CONTAINER-FLUID

The container-fluid class is also a *container*, but it sets the width to the full width of the screen.

Note: All the *bootstrap* classes will readjust themselves automatically as your screen size changes.

PAGE-HEADER

.PAGE-HEADER

The page-header adds space around the text, and enlarges the text inside of it.

Header

Note: The red color on the pictures serves to limit the division. You will not see it on your website.

```
<div
class="container">

<div class="page-
header">

<h1>Header</h1>

</div>
</div>
```

BUTTONS

There are several ways to use *bootstrap* buttons. You can either use the <a> *tag* and add a "btn" class, you can use the <button> *tag* in combination with the "btn" class, or the <input> *tag* in combination with the "btn" *tag*.

Example:

```
<a href="#" class="btn btn-default btn-sm" role="button">Button</a>

<button type="submit" href="#" class="btn btn-danger btn-md" role="button">Button</button>

<input href="#" class="btn btn-warning btn-lg" role="button" value="Button">
```

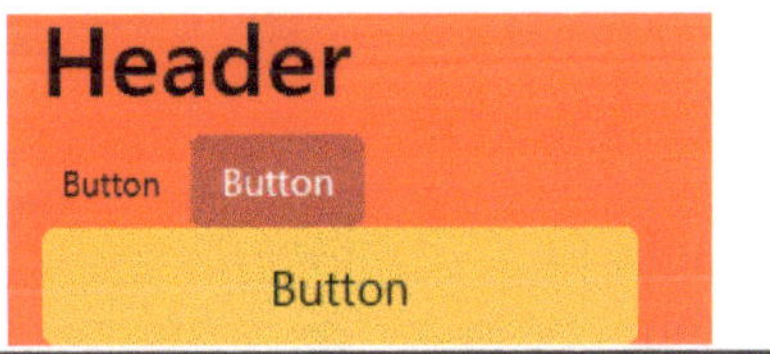

There are several ways you can change the buttons. You can change their colors and sizes.

To change the color of a button simply add one of the following classes.

`.btn`

Basic

`.btn-default`

Default

`.btn-primary`

Primary

`.btn-success`

Success

`.btn-info`

Info

`.btn-warning`

Warning

`.btn-warning`

Danger

`.btn-link`

Link

You can also change the size of your buttons.

```
.btn-lg
.btn-sm
.btn-xs
```

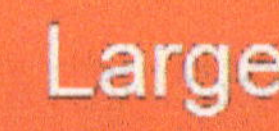

Normal

Small

XSmall

.btn-block

Button 1

If you want to disable a button, add the class ".disabled". The user will then not be able to click on this specific button.

`.disabled`

Disabled Button

GRID LAYOUTS / RESPONSIVE LAYOUTS

Let's create the root of a responsive bootstrap website. Start by adding a "line" inside the "*container*".

.ROW

The "row" element is invisible and serves as a *container* for the columns you will put inside of it.

.COL-

With the column class you can create up to 12 columns in a row. By placing a number after the ".col-" *value*, you determine the size it takes on the screen. If you want to, add three columns, you would have to divide 12 by three:

12 / 3 = 4

Add the class col-4.

Example:

```
<div
class="container">
<div class="row">
<div        class="col-
4">Text</div>
<div        class="col-
4">Text</div>
<div        class="col-
4">Text</div>
</div>
</div>
```

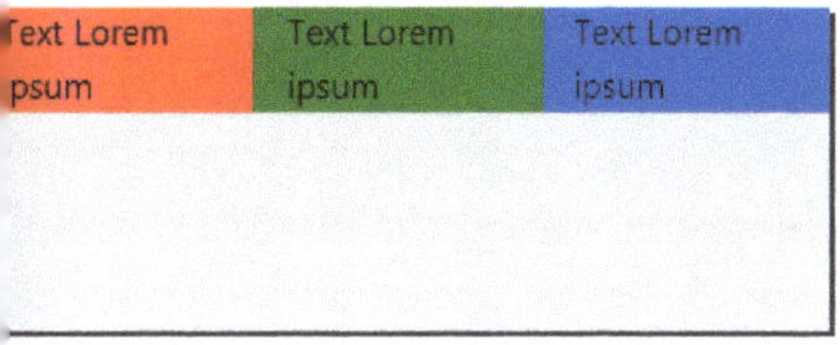

Text Lorem ipsum | Text Lorem ipsum | Text Lorem ipsum

As your screen gets smaller, you will encounter some problems. If you have a very small screen these columns will stay columns and will not adapt themselves to your phone.

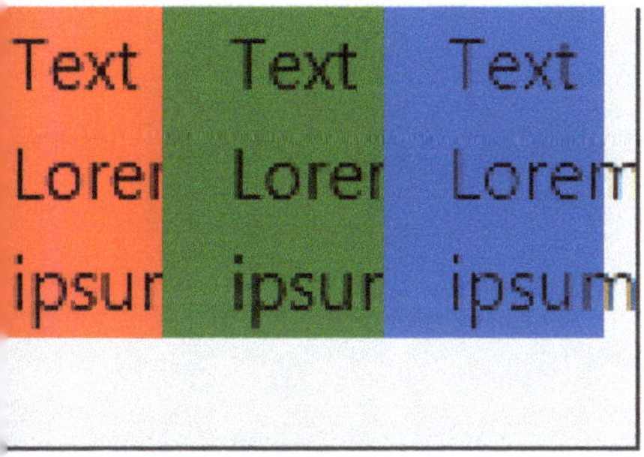

Text Lorem ipsum | Text Lorem ipsum | Text Lorem ipsum

To prevent this, add a short *attribute* that disables the column layout for small devices.

```
<div
class="container">
<div class="row">

<div    class="col-sm-
4"> Text </div>
<div    class="col-sm-
4"> Text </div>
<div    class="col-sm-
4"> Text </div>

</div>
</div>
```

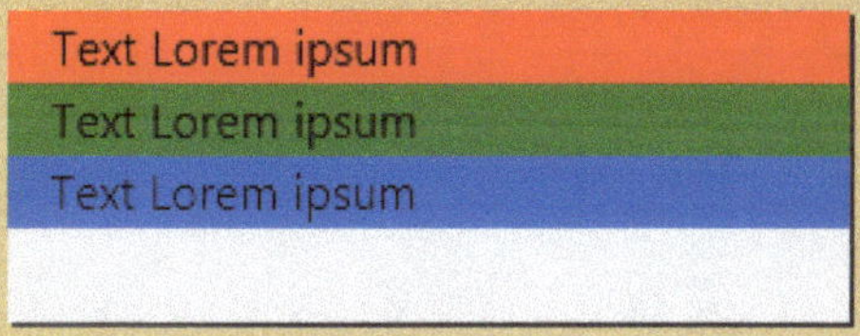

Text Lorem ipsum

Text Lorem ipsum

Text Lorem ipsum

You can add the **"sm"** *attribute* to disable columns for devices with a width smaller than **540px**. The **"md"** *attribute* for devices with a width smaller than **720px**. The **"lg"** *attribute* for devices with a width smaller than **960px** and smaller and the **"xl"** *attribute* for devices with a width smaller than **1200px**.

You might also want to hide elements on a specific screen size:

```
hidden-sm
hidden-md
hidden-lg
hidden-xl
```

ADDITIONAL USEFUL CLASSES

.D-BLOCK

The d-block class enables "display: block". It will take up the entire width of its *container*.

.D-NONE

D-none will set the "display" *property* to "none". It will hide your element and the space it occupies.

.D-FLEX

D-flex sets the "display" *property* to "flex".

Display flex will in most cases center its *child attribute* if the margin of the *child* is set to "auto".

.TEXT-CENTER

This class centers your text. It could also be aligned on the **left, right** or **justify**.

Lorem Ipsum is simply dummy text of the printing and typesetting industry. Lorem Ipsum has been the industry's standard dummy text ever since the 1500s, when an unknown printer took a galley of type and scrambled it to make a

Lorem Ipsum is simply dummy text of the printing and typesetting industry. Lorem Ipsum has been the industry's standard dummy text ever since the 1500s, when an unknown printer took a galley of type and scrambled it to make a

Lorem Ipsum is simply dummy text of the printing and typesetting industry. Lorem Ipsum has been the industry's standard dummy text ever since the 1500s, when an unknown printer took a galley of type and scrambled it to make a

Lorem Ipsum is simply dummy text of the printing and typesetting industry. Lorem Ipsum has been the industry's standard dummy text ever since the 1500s, when an unknown printer took a galley of type and scrambled it to make a

.ALIGN-ITEMS-STRETCH

"Align-items-stretch" allows you to stretch elements vertically in their *containers*. It is often used with flexboxes.

```
<div class="d-flex align-items-stretch">
<div class="p-2 border">Flex item 1</div>
<div class="p-2 border">Flex item 2</div>
<div class="p-2 border">Flex item 3</div>
</div>
```

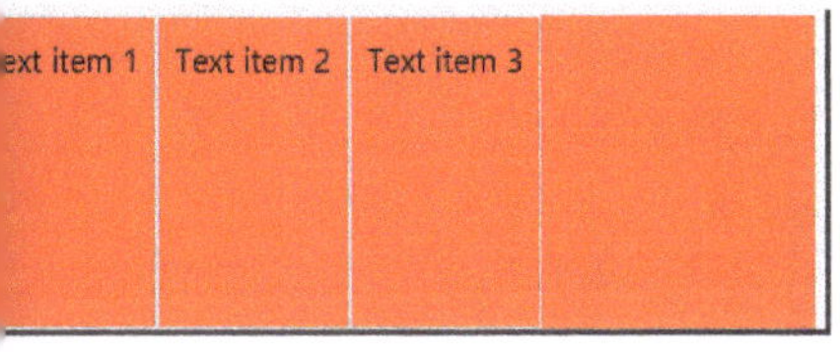

You can also align items at the **center**.

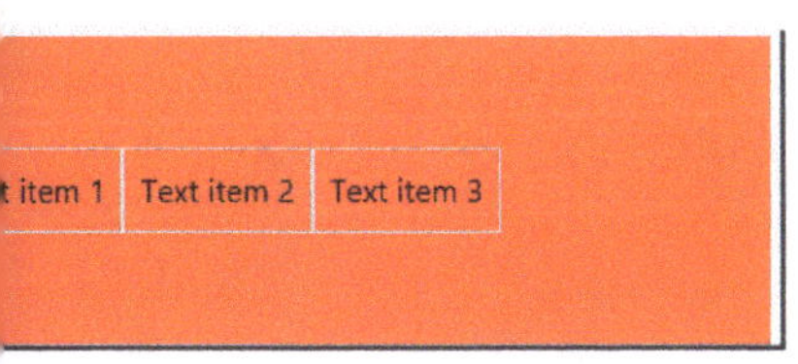

The "Align-items-stretch" class also allows you to align items at the **start** of a *container*.

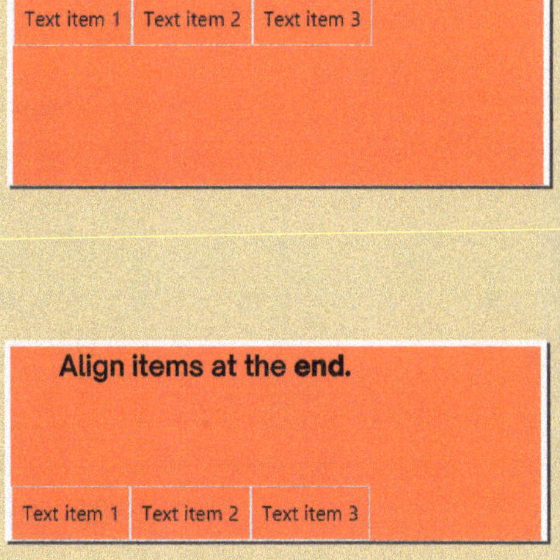

.JUSTIFY-CONTENT-CENTER

"Justify-content-center" lets you center the *child* of a flex element horizontally.

CSS STYLING WITH BOOTSTRAP

If you want to change the style of a *boostrap* class, you must change the file 'bootstrap.css'.

My First Site ▸ bootstrap-4.4.1-dist ▸ css

- bootstrap.css
- bootstrap.css.map
- bootstrap.min.css
- bootstrap.min.css.map
- bootstrap-grid.css
- bootstrap-grid.css.map
- bootstrap-grid.min.css
- bootstrap-grid.min.css.map
- bootstrap-reboot.css
- bootstrap-reboot.css.map
- bootstrap-reboot.min.css
- bootstrap-reboot.min.css.map

Open the file and use the "Control + F" shortcut on Windows or the "Command + F" shortcut on Mac and search for the class you want to edit.

CAROUSEL SLIDER

Bootstrap has some built in features. One of them is the carousel slider. Instead of showing a single large image at a time, carousels show multiple images in a row.

Start by adding either a background-image or a background color to the sliders.

```
<style>

.slide1,
.slide2,
.slide3 {

background: red;
height: 500px;

}
</style>
```

Inside of your *body* add a division with the class "carousel" and "slide". Also add a "data-ride" *attribute* with the *value* "carousel" and add an id.

```
<div id="carouselID"
class="carousel
slide" data-
ride="carousel">
```

```
   ...
<div>
```

Now create an *unordered list* with the class "carousel-indicators" and add three list items. These items should contain a "data-target" *attribute* with the *value* of the id you gave to your *container*. Include the "data-slide-to" *attribute* and use the *value* "0" for the first item, the *value* "1" for the second item and the *value* "2" for the last one.

```
<ul class="carousel-
indicators">

<li data-
target="#carouselID"
data-slide-to="0"
class="active"></li>

<li data-
target="#carouselID"
data-slide-to="1">
</li>

<li data-
target="#carouselID"
data-slide-to="2">
</li>

</ul>
```

Create the sliders by using the division "carousel-inner". Add the <div> "carousel-item active" and add two *child* divisions: "slide1" and "carousel-caption". In the last <div> add the text you want to appear on the slide.

```
<div class="slide1">
</div>

<div class="carousel-
caption">

<h1>Headline</h1>

<p>Lorem ipsum Lorem
ipsum Lorem ipsum
Lorem ipsum</p>

<p><a href="#"
class="btn btn-
primary btn-
sm">Button</a></p>

</div>
```

Repeat this step three times to get three sliders.

Note: You have to change the class "slide1" to the corresponding number. You also have to remove the class "active" from the other "carousel items".

```
<div class="carousel-
inner">

<div class="carousel-
item active">

<div class="slide1">
</div>
<div class="carousel-
caption">

<h1>Headline</h1>

<p>Lorem ipsum Lorem
ipsum Lorem ipsum
Lorem ipsum</p>

<p><a href="#"
class="btn btn-
primary btn-
sm">Button</a></p>

</div>
</div>

<div class="carousel-
item">

<div class="slide2">
</div>
<div class="carousel-
caption">

<h1>Headline2</h1>

<p>Lorem ipsum Lorem
ipsum Lorem ipsum
Lorem ipsum</p>

</div>
</div>

<div class="carousel-
item">

<div class="slide3">
</div>
<div class="carousel-
caption">

<h1>Headline3</h1>

<p>Lorem ipsum Lorem
ipsum Lorem ipsum
Lorem ipsum</p>

</div>
</div>

</div>
```

The last step is to add the left and right arrows. Use the <a> *tag* in combination with the class "carousel-control-prev". Include the *href attribute* with the *value* of your carousel id and add the data-slide *attribute* with the *value* "prev".

Inside your <a> *tag* add the <span> *tag* with the class "carousel-control-prev-icon". Repeat this step while changing the "prev" *values* to "next."

```
<a class="carousel-
control-prev"
href="#carouselID"
data-slide="prev">

<span
class="carousel-
control-prev-icon">
</span>

</a>

<a class="carousel-
control-next"
href="#carouselID"
data-slide="next">

<span
class="carousel-
control-next-icon">

</span>

</a>
```

AOS

Aos is an open source scrolling *library*. It allows you to change the scrolling behavior of certain elements as you scroll.

To get *Aos* go to michalsnik.github.io/aos/ use the two CDN sources or download the package and link the *CSS* source in your *header* and the js source at the end of your *body*.

Then add the following code after the script *tag* you have just added:

```
<script>
  AOS.init();
</script>
```

You have now successfully added the *Aos plugin*. To test it, simply create several divisions and give them a width, height and background color.

```
<div class="d1" data-
aos="fade-up"></div>
<div class="d1" data-
aos="fade-up"></div>
<div class="d1" data-
aos="fade-up"></div>
<div class="d1" data-
aos="fade-up"></div>
<div class="d1" data-
aos="fade-up"></div>
<div class="d1" data-
aos="fade-up"></div>
<div class="d1" data-
aos="fade-up"></div>
<div class="d1" data-
aos="fade-up"></div>
<div class="d1" data-
aos="fade-up"></div>

.d1 {
  background: red;
  height: 150px;
  width: 150px;
  display: block;
  margin: 10px;
}
```

Don't forget to include the aos="fade-up" *attribute* which is shown in bold above.

FANCYBOX

Fancybox is a *JavaScript library* used to present photos and videos responsively.

Download the *library* at fancyapps.com/fancybox/3/. Extract the package in your folder and add the following line in your *head* to import the *library*:

```
<link rel="stylesheet" href="fancybox-master/dist/jquery.fancybox.css">
```

Use the following line to import the *JavaScript* files:

```
<link
rel="stylesheet"
href="fancybox-
master/dist/jquery.fancybox.js">
```

Give *fancybox* a try with the following code:

```
<a data-
fancybox="gallery"
href="imgs/wallpaper.jpg"><img
src="imgs/wallpaper.jpg"></a>
<a data-
fancybox="gallery"
href="imgs/wallpaper2.jpg"><img
src="imgs/wallpaper2.jpg"></a>

img {
  background: red;
  width: 100px;
  height: 100px;
}
```

SLICKNAV

Go to pluginsroom.com /plugins/ slicknav-mobile-menu and download *slicknav*. Extract the package and copy it into your website folder. Include the following code in the *head* of your index:

```
<link
rel="stylesheet"
href="slickn av-
mobile-
menu/css/slicknav.mi
n.css">
```

Add this line at the bottom of your *body*:

```
<script
src="slicknav-mobile-
menu/js/jquery.slickn
av.min.js"></script>
```

In the next chapter you will learn how to use *slicknav* in detail. When you begin to create your mobile navigation menu, you will implement this tool with *HTML*, *CSS* and *JavaScript*.

ACTION STEPS

1. Remove the content inside the section of your *body*.
2. Create 10 divisions and style them with a width, height and background-color.
3. Add a margin
4. Link *Aos* in case you didn't do so already
5. Add at least 3 different data-aos *properties*

YOUR HTML CODE:

```
...
<head>
  <link rel="stylesheet" href="aos-
  master/dist/aos.css">
</head>

<body>

  <header>
    <nav></nav>
  </header>

  <main>
    <section>

      <div class="d1" data-aos="fade-up">
      </div>
      <div class="d1" data-aos="fade-up">
      </div>
      <div class="d1" data-aos="fade-up">
      </div>
      <div class="d1" data-aos="fade-up">
      </div>
      <div class="d1" data-aos="flip-down">
      </div>
      <div class="d1" data-aos="flip-down">
      </div>
```

```
        <div class="d1" data-aos="flip-down">
        </div>
        <div  class="d1"  data-aos="zoom-in-
        right"></div>
        <div  class="d1"  data-aos="zoom-in-
        right"></div>
        <div  class="d1"  data-aos="zoom-in-
        right"></div>

      </section>
    </main>

    <footer></footer>

    <script      src="aos-master/dist/aos.js">
    </script>

    <script>
      AOS.init();
    </script>

</body>
```

YOUR CSS CODE:

```
.d1 {
  background: red;
  height: 150px;
  width: 150px;
  display: block;
  margin: 10px;
}
```

CREATING YOUR FIRST WEBSITE

5.

ROBINKBR.COM

WHAT WE WILL PROGRAM

Go to robinkbr.com/demo to see a live demo of the site you are about to create.

The creation process is divided into 4 major parts:

1. *Header*
2. *Main* content (which is subdivided into 4 parts)
- Top picture
- Photo section
- Blog area
- Video section
3. *Footer*
4. *Preloader*

Header:

Top picture:

Photo section:

Blog area:

My blog

Newest

My first blog post

September 1, 1998 by Robin

My second blog post

August 1, 20222 by Robin

My third blog post

November 6, 3021 by Robin

Video Section:

My Story

Lorem Ipsum is simply dummy text of the printing and typesetting industry. Lorem Ipsum has been the industry's standard dummy text ever since the 1500s, when an unknown printer took a galley of type and scrambled it to make a type specimen book. It has survived not only five centuries, but also the leap into electronic typesetting, remaining essentially unchanged.

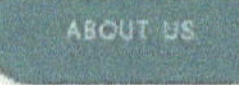

Footer:

Preloader:

THE FIRST STEPS

For your website to start properly, you need to make sure that everything is correct. At this point, your "index.html" <head> *tag* should contain :

- Meta - utf
- Title
- Keywords, description
- Viewport
- Favicon link
- JQuery
- Bootstrap
- Aos
- Fancybox
- Slicknav
- Your 'style.css' sheet

Your <body> should **only** include the following *tags*:

- header
- main
- footer

At the end of your *body* you must include the following scripts:
- Bootstrap
- Aos
- Fancybox
- Slicknav

Delete all *declarations* from your "style.css" file and make your stylesheet look empty.

Your website folder should look like this:

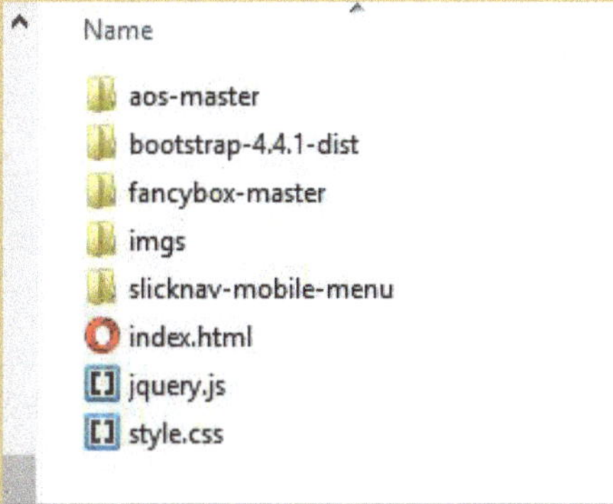

During the creation of your website, there will be passages where you will need *JavaScript*. To simplify the process, create a "script.js" file and add it to your website folder. Link this file at the bottom of your <body>.

YOUR 'INDEX.HTML' FILE

```
<!doctype html>
<html>

<head>

  <meta charset="UTF-8">

  <title>Robin</title>

  <meta name="keywords"
  content="HTML,CSS,JavaScript">
  <meta name="author" content="Robin">
  <meta name="description" content="My First
  HTML Website!">

  <meta name="viewport"
  content="width=device-width, initial-
  scale=1.0">

  <!--Favicons-->
  <link rel="apple-touchicon" sizes="180x180"
  href="imgs/apple-touch-icon.png">
  <link rel="icon" type="image/png"
  sizes="32x32" href="imgs/favicon-
  32x32.png">
  <link rel="icon" type="image/png"
  sizes="16x16" href="imgs/favicon-
  16x16.png">
  <link                        rel="manifest"
  href="/site.webmanifest">

  <!--JQuery-->
  <script src="jquery.js"></script>
```

```
    <!--Bootstrap-->
    <link    rel="stylesheet"    href="bootstrap-
    4.4.1-dist/css/bootstrap.css">

    <!--AOS-->
    <link        rel="stylesheet"        href="aos-
    master/dist/aos.css">

    <!--Fancybox-->
    <link    rel="stylesheet"    href="fancybox-
    master/dist/jquery.fancybox.css">

    <!--Slicknav-->
    <link    rel="stylesheet"    href="slicknav-
    mobile-menu/css/slicknav.css">


    <!--Style.css-->
    <link rel="stylesheet" href="style.css">

</head>

<body>

    <header></header>

    <main></main>

    <footer></footer>

    <!--Bootstrap-->
    <script                src="bootstrap-4.4.1-
    dist/js/bootstrap.js"></script>
```

```html
    <!--Bootstrap-->
    <script                src="bootstrap-4.4.1-
    dist/js/bootstrap.js"></script>

    <!--AOS-->
    <script       src="aos-master/dist/aos.js">
    </script>

    <!--Fancybox-->
    <script                       src="fancybox-
    master/dist/jquery.fancybox.js"></script>

    <!--Slicknav-->
    <script                src="slicknav-mobile-
    menu/js/jquery.slicknav.min.js"></script>

    <!--script.js-->
    <script src="script.js"></script>

  </body>

  </html>
```

START

HTML tags have standard *CSS properties*. Some of these *properties* do not match the design. You will need to make some adjustments.

In your 'style.css' file add a *variable* to the main color of your site. In the example site at robinkbr.com/demo the main color is 'cadetblue':

```
:root {
  --main-color:
  cadetblue;
}
```

Then import two specific fonts that are not included per default: "Josefin Sans", "Sacramento" and "Sulphur Point".

```
@import
url(https://fonts.
googleapis.com/css?
family
=Josefin+Sans:300,400
,500,600,700|Sacramen
to|Sulphur+Point:400,
700&display=swap);
```

Add the following font to your *body* and set it to bold.

```
body {
  font-family:
  "Sulphur    Point",
  sans-serif;
  font-weight: 400;
}
```

If the font "Sulphur Point" is not able to load, your browser will use the font "sans-serif" which is always available. Also change the font of the elements <h1> to <h6> and give them a dark color. Change the margin to "auto" so that the headlines get centered:

```
h1, h2, h3, h4, h5,
h6 {
  font-family:
  "Sulphur    Point",
  sans-serif;
  color: #1c1930;
  margin-top: 0;
}
```

Now change the font of every paragraph to "Sulphur Point", add a dark color, but not the same as before and change the font-size to 16px, the line-height to 30px and show the text in bold.

```
p {
  font-family:
  "Sulphur    Point",
  sans-serif;
  color: #10285d;
  font-size: 16px;
  line-height: 30px;
  font-weight: 400;
}
```

The line height *property* defines the height between two lines of a paragraph.

You may have noticed that the links you add to your website, get a bluish color and standard underlining. If you don't like it, change their style by adding a white color to all links on your site:

```
a {
  color: #fff;
}
```

Also change the color of your hovered links. To do this, remove the old underline and add the "text-decoration" *proper-ty*. Set the *value* to "none". This will permanently remove the underline.

```
a:hover {
  color: white;
  text-decoration:
  none;
}
```

As you will create a navigation menu, you will need to create a list. Edit the list items by removing the default margin, padding and bullet points.

```
ul {
  margin: 0;
  padding: 0;
}

li {
  list-style: none;
}
```

The list style *property* defines the style of the bullet points in your list.. You could also set it to:

◦ circle
▪ square
III. upper-roman
d. lower-alpha

YOUR 'STYLE.CSS' FILE

```
@import
url(https://fonts.googleapis.com/css?
family=Josefin+Sans:300,400,500,600,700|Sacr
amento|Sulphur+Point:400,700&display=swap);

/*----------------Adjustments---------------
-*/

:root {
  --main-color: cadetblue;
}

body {
  font-family: "Sulphur Point", sans-serif;
  font-weight: 400;
}

h1, h2, h3, h4, h5, h6 {
  font-family: "Sulphur Point", sans-serif;
  color: #1c1930;
  margin-top: 0;
}

p {
  font-family: "Sulphur Point", sans-serif;
  color: #10285d;
  font-size: 16px;
  line-height: 30px;
  font-weight: 400;
}
```

```css
a {
  color: #fff;
}

a:hover {
  color: #fff;
  text-decoration: none;
}

ul {
  margin: 0;
  padding: 0;
}

li {
  list-style: none;
}
```

HEADER

Let's now edit your *HTML* code. In your *header* create a division. Give it a class and an id. On the demo site the class "header-area" and the id "top" are used. I recommend you to use the same *values*. It will be easier for you since you are going to use them again later on in *CSS*.

Create a subdivision and classify it as "head-down". This will be the area that is fixed at the top of your screen when you scroll.

Then create a third division inside of the last one you created. This division will be the bootstrap *container* for our *header*. Class it as "container-fluid".

Now create a division "row" and give it a second class: "align-items-center". Every text inside this division will be centered.

```
<div class="header-area" id="top">

<div class="header-bottom">

<div
class="container-fluid">

<div class="row
align-items-center">

</div>
</div>
</div>
</div>
```

In your row create 3 columns. The first column needs to have the classes col-xl-2, col-lg-2 and col-md-1.

The second column should have the classes col-xl-10, col-lg-10 and col-md-8.

Each row can only have a maximum of 12 columns. However, the third column will only be visible on mobile phones. It will replace the other two and become the navigation bar for mobile devices.

```
<div class="col-xl-2 col-lg-2 col-md-1">
</div>

<div class="col-xl-10 col-lg-10 col-md-8">
</div>

<div class="col-12">
</div>
```

Continue by adding a logo. Inside the first column you created (col-xl-2 col-lg-2 col-md-1), add a "Logo" division. Create a link and use 'index.html' as the "href" *value*. Write down the text you want to have as logo.

```
<div class="logo"> <a
href="https://www.rob
inkbr.com">Robin</a>
</div>
```

In the second column create a division with the classes: "main-menu", "d-none", "d-lg-block". "Main menu" is the class you will use to customize the element. d-none makes it invisible for small screen devices and d-lg-block makes it reappear for large screens.

In this division add the <nav> *tag* and create a list inside of it.

```
<ul id="navigation">
<li><a
href="#top">Home</a>
</li>

<li><a
href="#section-
photos">Phots</a>
</li>

<li><a href="#blog-
section">Blog</a>
</li>

<li><a href="#about-
section">About</a>
  <ul
  class="submenu">
  <li><a
  href="#">Blog</a>
  </li>
  <li><a
  href="#">Blog
  Post</a></li>
  <li><a
  href="#">Details</a
  ></li>
  </ul>
</li>

<li class="contact">
<a
href="#">Contact</a>
</li>
</ul>
```

The bold code on the previous page shows a sub menu. If you like you can use one on your website.

Additionally the very last list item has a class attached to it. It represents the button you will design in *CSS*.

The ids you see as an "href" *value* stand for the website sections you will create. Every section gets an id and when you click on the navigation links your site will scroll automatically to the desired section. You might also want to add an external website or a second site you created. If you do, simply change the href="" *attribute*.

In the last column of your *header*, simply add a division with the class "mobile-menu d-lg-none". This is the mobile menu that will not appear on large screens.

YOUR HTML CODE

```
<header>

  <div class="header-area" id="top">

    <div class="header-bottom">
      <div class="container-fluid">
        <div class="row align-items-
        center">

          <div class="col-xl-2 col-lg-2
          col-md-1">
            <div class="logo">
              <a
              href="https://www.robinkbr.co
              m">Robin</a>
            </div>
          </div>

          <div class="col-xl-10 col-lg-10
          col-md-8">
            <div class="main-menu d-none d-
            lg-block">
              <nav>
                <ul id="navigation">
                <li><a href="#top">Home</a>
                </li>
                <li><a href="#section-
                photos">Phots</a></li>
                <li><a href="#blog-
                section">Blog</a></li>
```

```
                    <li><a href="#about-
                    section">About</a>

                    <ul class="submenu">
                    <li><a href="#">Blog</a>
                    </li>
                    <li><a href="#">Blog
                    Post</a></li>
                    <li><a href="#">Details</a>
                    </li>
                    </ul>

                    </li>
                    <li class="contact"><a
                    href="#">Contact</a></li>
                    </ul>
                  </nav>
                </div>
              </div>

              <div class="col-12">
                <div class="mobile_menu d-lg-
                none"></div>
              </div>

            </div>
          </div>
        </div>
      </div>

    </header>
```

Now edit the *CSS* of your *header*. For the overall *container* called "header-area" add an absolute position, so that the *header* does not get affected by the other elements on the screen. Then you need to include the top *property* with the *value* 0 and the left and right *property* with the *value* 0. Finally, add "z-index": 9", because the navigation bar must be displayed in the foreground.

For the "header-bottom" class add a top and bottom padding of 0 and a left and right padding of 90px. You will see how it adds some spacing on both sides of the navigation.

```
.header-area {
  position: absolute;
  top: 0;
  right: 0;
  left: 0;
  z-index: 9
}

.header-area .header-
bottom {
  padding: 0 90px
}
```

Since the "header-area" and "header-bottom" classes are not a part of *Bootstrap* you need to adjust them for mobile devices manually:

Add a media query for the following screen sizes:

- 1200px-1600px
- 992px-1199px
- 768px-991px
- 576px-991px
- 576px-767px
- 575px

```
@media only screen
and (min-
width:1200px) and
(max-width:1600px) {
.header-area .header-
bottom {
  padding: 0 20px;
}
}

@media only screen
and (min-width:992px)
and (max-
width:1199px) {
.header-area .header-
bottom {
  padding: 0 20px;
}
}
```

```
@media only screen
and (min-width:768px)
and (max-width:991px)
{

.header-area .header-
bottom {
  padding: 22px 50px;
}
}

@media only screen
and (min-width:576px)
and (max-width:767px)
{
.header-area .header-
bottom {
  padding: 22px 20px;
}
}

@media (max-
width:575px) {
.header-area .header-
bottom {
  padding: 22px 20px;
}
}
```

Add the *selector* '.sticky-bar' to your stylesheet and set its position to fixed. When you scroll down it will be the division that stays on top of the page to show the navigation menu. You did not add this class to your *HTML*, yet it will add itself through a *JavaScript* passage as soon as the user scrolls.

Add the *declarations* "width: 100%", "z-index: 9999" and add a dark background.

```
.sticky-bar {
  position: fixed;
  width: 100%;
  z-index: 9999;
}
```

Also add a slight shadow underneath the *header* to do so add the following code:

```
-webkit-box-shadow: 0
10px 15px rgba(25,
25, 25, .1);
box-shadow: 0 10px
15px rgba(25, 25, 25,
.1);
```

The webkit preposition is used when adding a newer not yet established *property*. It is a fallback for the browsers, Chrome and Safari.

Now edit your logo by adding a font-size of 35px and set the font-family as 'Sacramento', cursive.

YOUR CSS CODE

```
/*------------------Header------------------
*/

.header-area {
  position: absolute;
  top: 0;
  right: 0;
  left: 0;
  z-index: 9;
}

.header-area .header-bottom {
  padding: 0 90px;
}

@media only screen and (min-width:1200px)
and (max-width:1600px) {
.header-area .header-bottom {
  padding: 0 20px;
}
}

@media only screen and (min-width:992px) and
(max-width:1199px) {
.header-area .header-bottom {
  padding: 0 20px;
}
}
```

```
@media only screen and (min-width:768px) and
(max-width:991px) {
.header-area .header-bottom {
  padding: 22px 50px;
}
}

@media only screen and (min-width:576px) and
(max-width:767px) {
.header-area .header-bottom {
  padding: 22px 20px;
}
}

@media (max-width:575px) {
.header-area .header-bottom {
  padding: 22px 20px;
}
}

.sticky-bar {
  position: fixed;
  width: 100%;
  z-index: 9999;
  -webkit-box-shadow: 0 10px 15px rgba(25,
  25, 25, .1);
  box-shadow: 0 10px 15px rgba(25, 25, 25,
  .1);
  background: #010E21;
}

.logo {
  font-size: 35px;
  font-family: "Sacramento", cursive;
}
```

You will now edit the style of the main menu links. To do this, you need to let them float on the right.

As you scroll, the text size of the *header* must be reduced. Go to robinkbr.com/demo - scroll a little and look at the *header*. To get this result, add the following line:

```
.header-bottom.sticky-bar .main-menu ul > li > a {
  padding: 27px 13px
}
```

It is necessary to remove the space between the ".header-bottom" class and the ".sticky-bar" class. The browser will then recognize that it is the same division to which a second class has been added.

Add the "display: inline-block" *declaration* to the list *attributes* of the main menu so they show up side by side. Also add a relative position and a z-index of 1.

```
.main-menu ul li {
  display: inline-block;
  position: relative;
  z-index: 1
}
```

As soon as you are finished, edit the links in the *header* navigation. Add a white color, display the text in bold, set the padding to 39px on the top and bottom and 27px on the left and right. Set the display *property* to block, the font size to 16px and add a *property* called transition. Set it to "all .3s ease-out 0s".

Your browser will then be able to switch smoothly between the two padding options you have defined for the *header* text.

You could also have used the *value* "padding" instead of "all" and the result would have been the same. The transition would then only apply to the "padding" *attribute* and not to "all" *attributes*.

The *value* ".3s" means that it will take 0.3 seconds to complete the transition.

The type of transition is facilitated and the delav is

ease out and the delay is 0.

For the transition *property* you will need to add some additional *vendor prefixes.*

The whole *rule set* looks like this:

```
.main-menu ul li a {
  color: #fff;
  font-weight: 500;
  padding: 39px 27px;
  display: block;
  font-size: 16px;
  -webkit-transition:
  all .3s ease-out
  0s;
  -moz-transition:
  all .3s ease-out
  0s;
  -ms-transition: all
  .3s ease-out 0s;
  -o-transition: all
  .3s ease-out 0s;
  transition: all .3s
  ease-out 0s;
}
```

The *vendor prefix* -moz- is used for Mozilla Firefox, -ms- for Internet Explorer and -o- for Opera.

Now you need to adjust the padding for smaller screens:

```
@media only screen
and (min-width:992px)
and (max-
width:1199px) {
.main-menu ul li a {
padding: 39px 15px;
}
}

@media only screen
and (min-
width:1200px) and
(max-width:1380px) {
.main-menu ul li a {
  padding: 39px 17px;
}
}
```

Also edit the color of the menu links as you hover over them:

```
.main-menu ul
li:hover > a {
  color: var(--main-
  color);
}
```

Remember to use the *variable* you created beforehand.

Also create a button at the top of the page. To do this, add the class "Contact" as a *selector* and target only the link it contains. Change the background color to the default color of your website, create rounded corners, add a top and bottom padding of 14px and a left and right padding of 33px. Set the left and right margin to 11px, change its color to white and edit the color when hovered to white.

```
.header-area .main-
menu ul li.contact >
a {
  background: var(--
  main-color);
  border-radius:
  30px;
  padding: 14px 33px;
  margin: 0 11px;
}

.header-area .main-
menu ul li.contact >
a:hover {
  color: #fff;
}
```

The preselectors such as ".header-area .main-menu" are necessary in order to disable these *properties* on mobile devices.

If you added a submenu in *HTML* you also need to style it.

Set the position to absolute and give it a limited width. I recommend using 170px. Set the background to white. Add the top *property* with a *value* of 120% so that it can be faded in from the bottom to the top and set the visibility and opacity to hidden and 0.

Also add a slight box shadow and a 17px fill for top and bottom. Add a top border of 5px with your default color.

```
.main-menu ul
ul.submenu {
  position: absolute;
  width: 170px;
  background: #fff;
  top: 120%;
  visibility: hidden;
  opacity: 0;
  -webkit-box-shadow:
  0 0 10px 3px
  rgba(0, 0, 0, .05);
  box-shadow: 0 0
  10px 3px rgba(0, 0,
  0, .05);
  padding: 17px 0;
  border-top: 5px
  solid var(--main-
  color);
  -webkit-transition:
```

```
    all .3s ease-out
    0s;
    -moz-transition:
    all .3s ease-out
    0s;
    -ms-transition:
    all .3s ease-out
    0s;
    -o-transition: all
    .3s ease-out 0s;
    transition: all
    .3s ease-out 0s
}
```

Now change the links on the submenu:

```
.main-menu ul
ul.submenu > li {
  margin-left: 7px;
  display: block;
}

.main-menu ul
ul.submenu > li > a {
  padding: 6px 10px;
  font-size: 16px;
  color: #0b1c39;
  text-transform:
  capitalize;
}

.main-menu ul
ul.submenu > li >
a:hover {
  color: var(--main-
  color);
  background: 0 0;
}
```

The display block *declaration* allows the list elements to show up beneath each other. The color of the links is also important since you cannot see them with a white background.

The other *properties* are more a matter of taste.

The last *rule set* you need to add to our *header* is the visible submenu:

```
.main-menu ul >
li:hover > ul.submenu
{
  visibility: visible
  !important;
  opacity: 1
  !important;
  top: 100%
  !important;
  z-index: 99;
}
```

This *property* is applied to the submenu when you move the mouse over the link in the *header*. It simply makes it visible and sets the top *property* to 100%. Since you have previously added a transition *property*, it will fade up from the bottom to the top.

YOUR CSS CODE

```
/*--main menu--*/

.main-menu {
  float: right;
}

.header-bottom.sticky-bar .main-menu ul > li
> a {
  padding: 27px 13px;
}

.main-menu ul li {
  display: inline-block;
  position: relative;
  z-index: 1;
}

.main-menu ul li a {
  color: #fff;
  font-weight: 500;
  padding: 39px 27px;
  display: block;
  font-size: 16px;
  -webkit-transition: all .3s ease-out 0s;
  -moz-transition: all .3s ease-out 0s;
  -ms-transition: all .3s ease-out 0s;
  -o-transition: all .3s ease-out 0s;
  transition: all .3s ease-out 0s;
}
```

```
@media only screen and (min-width:992px) and
(max-width:1199px) {
.main-menu ul li a {
  padding: 39px 15px;
}
}

@media only screen and (min-width:1200px)
and (max-width:1380px) {
.main-menu ul li a {
  padding: 39px 17px;
}
}

.main-menu ul li:hover > a {
  color: var(--main-color);
}

.header-area .main-menu ul li.contact > a {
  background: var(--main-color);
  border-radius: 30px;
  padding: 14px 33px;
  margin: 0 11px;
}

.header-area .main-menu ul li.contact >
a:hover {
  color: #fff;
}

.main-menu ul ul.submenu {
  position: absolute;
  width: 170px;
  background: #fff;
  top: 120%;
  visibility: hidden;
  opacity: 0;
```

```
    -webkit-box-shadow: 0 0 10px 3px rgba(0, 0,
    0, .05);
    box-shadow: 0 0 10px 3px rgba(0, 0, 0, .05);
    padding: 17px 0;
    border-top: 5px solid var(--main-color);
    -webkit-transition: all .3s ease-out 0s;
    -moz-transition: all .3s ease-out 0s;
    -ms-transition: all .3s ease-out 0s;
    -o-transition: all .3s ease-out 0s;
    transition: all .3s ease-out 0s;
}

.main-menu ul ul.submenu > li {
    margin-left: 7px;
    display: block;
}

.main-menu ul ul.submenu > li > a {
    padding: 6px 10px;
    font-size: 16px;
    color: #0b1c39;
    text-transform: capitalize;
}

.main-menu ul ul.submenu > li > a:hover {
    color: var(--main-color);
    background: 0 0;
}

.main-menu ul > li:hover > ul.submenu {
    visibility: visible;
    opacity: 1;
    top: 100%;
    z-index: 99;
}

/*-----------------End Header---------------
--*/
```

Now you need to change the mobile menu.

Since you installed Slicknav, the mobile menu is already working and you only need to make slight style adjustments.

The default *attributes* of the "mobile_menu" are a width of 96% and right 10%. Change this to width 100% and right 0.

```
.mobile_menu {
  right: 0;
  width: 100%;
}
```

The following classes are not included in you "index.html" file. However, they are added automatically via *Slicknav*.

```
.mobile_menu
.slicknav_menu {
  margin-top: 16px;
}
```

The *Slicknav* menu is the overall *container* of all the *Slicknav* elements. You have just modified the element so that it appears lower.

The following code adjusts the hovered links to have the main color.

```
.mobile_menu
.slicknav_menu
.slicknav_nav a:hover
{
  color: var(--main-
  color);
}
```

Change the menu icon to fit the color theme.

```
.mobile_menu
.slicknav_menu
.slicknav_icon-bar {
  background-color:
  var(--main-color);
}
```

You should also move the overall menu icon to the top:

```
.mobile_menu
.slicknav_btn {
  top: -48px
}
```

The last thing you need to change is the margin of the mobile navigation area:

```
.mobile_menu
.slicknav_nav {
  margin-top: 0;
}
```

YOUR CSS CODE

```
/*----------------Mobile Menu--------------
*/

.mobile_menu {
  position: absolute;
  right: 0;
  width: 100%;
  z-index: 99;
}

.mobile_menu .slicknav_menu {
  margin-top: 16px;
}

.mobile_menu .slicknav_menu .slicknav_nav
a:hover {
  color: var(--main-color);
}

.mobile_menu .slicknav_menu .slicknav_icon-bar
{
  background-color: var(--main-color);
}

.mobile_menu .slicknav_btn {
  top: -48px;
}

.mobile_menu .slicknav_nav {
  margin-top: 0;
}

/*-------------End Mobile Menu-------------
*/
```

HEADER SCRIPT

At this point you have a navigation bar for your computer screen. You still need to add the ***JavaScript*** for your mobile menu and for the sticky desktop bar.

Open your 'script.js' file and add the following code:

```
$(document).ready(function (e) {

});
```

This is a jQuery function that allows your browser to execute the code only after your elements are ready or 'loaded'.

QUICK JQUERY GUIDE

JQuery works with *selecotrs* and *actions*.

```
$(selector).action()
```

You can use a class, an id or a *tag* name as a *selector*.

Example:

```
$(".mydiv").click(function(){
   $("p").css("font-size", 50px");
});
```

In the example above, the divisions with the class "mydiv" are the *selectors* and as you click on them all the paragraphs on your site get a 50px font size.

".css" is the *event*. Some other useful events include:

- scrollTop
- scrollBottom
- removeClass
- addClass
- fadeOut
- fadeIn
- click
- hover

Let's begin our jQuery road by adding the "sticky-bar" class to your *header*. Add this line in your $(document).ready function to define the scrolling event of your page:

```
$(window).on("scroll",
function () {

});
```

Every time the user scrolls, the browser checks one of the two cases you are about to add.

If the user scrolls more than 400 pixels, the sticky bar is displayed. If not, the bar remains hidden:

```
if
($(window).scrollTop(
) < 400) {
  $(".header-
  bottom").removeClas
  s("sticky-bar");
} else {
  $(".header-
  bottom").addClass("
  sticky-bar");
}
```

Now change the mobile navigation menu. *Slicknav* already designed everything. You just have to define the names of our navigation menu:

```
var nav =
$("ul#navigation");
nav.length &&
nav.slicknav({
  prependTo:
  ".mobile_menu",
  closedSymbol: "+",
  openedSymbol: "-"
});
```

In the code above the name of the navigation menu is "#navigation". Add this name as a variable.

You also need to define the mobile menu so that *Slicknav* can import the links from your desktop menu into the mobile menu. In this case the name is ".mobile_menu".

If you open your 'index.html' file in a browser and reduce the width of your browser window until you see the mobile menu, you may notice the ugly arrow inside this menu.

Change that and use the "+" and "-" sign to make it look modern.

YOUR JAVASCRIPT CODE

```
$(document).ready(function (e) {

/* sticky */

$(window).on("scroll", function () {
  if ($(window).scrollTop() < 400) {
    $(".header-bottom").removeClass("sticky-
    bar")
  } else {
    $(".header-bottom").addClass("sticky-
    bar")
  }
});


/* slick Nav */

var nav = $("ul#navigation");
nav.length && nav.slicknav({
  prependTo: ".mobile_menu",
  closedSymbol: "+",
  openedSymbol: "-"
});

});
```

MAIN

TOP IMAGE

Congratulations on finishing your first *HTML* section. If you want to see what you have created, just open the "index.html" file in your browser.

You are now going to create the large image at the top of your website.

Inside your <main> *tag* create a <section>, classify it as "slider-area" and "hero-overly". This will be the section where you will add your background image.

In this section, create a div and give it the classes "slider-height", "hero-overly", "d-flex" and "align-items-center". This will be a darken overlay for your picture. It will make your site look more professional.

Now add a div with the class "*container*" inside of the last division you created.

Inside of this same *container* create a *Bootstrap* row and add the class "justify-content-center".

In your row you will obviously append a column: "col-xl-8 col-lg-9".

Now create a *container* for your headings: "header_ caption".

Also add the headlines with a span and an <h1> *tag* inside of them.

```
<section
class="slider-area
hero-overly">

<div class="hero-
overly slider-height
d-flex align-items-
center">

<div
class="container">

<div class="row
justify-content-
center">
```

```
<div class="col-xl-8
col-lg-9">

<div
class="header_capti
on">

<span>Welcome</span>

<h1>Learn HTML &
CSS</h1>

</div>
</div>
</div>
</div>
</div>
</section>
```

Now create an image to your *CSS*. All you need is a background image that you insert as your background.

For the overall *container* just add the image:

```
.slider-area {
  background-image:
  url(imgs/wallpaper.
  jpg);
  background-size:
  cover;
  background-repeat:
  no-repeat;
}
```

For the slider-height class add the min-height *property*. This *property* sets a minimum height for an element. If the content is smaller than the minimum height, this *declaration* is applied and prevents the content from shrinking further.

You also have to disable background repeat, set the background position to center and the background size to cover.

```
.slider-height {
  min-height: 890px;
  background-repeat:
  no-repeat;
  background-
  position: center
  center;
  background-size:
  cover;
}
```

Also append the *media queries* to make the height responsive.

```
@media only screen and
(min-width:992px) and
(max-width:1199px) {
.slider-height {
  min-height: 680px;
}
```

```
}

@media only screen
and (min-width:768px)
and (max-width:991px)
{
.slider-height {
  min-height: 600px;
}
}

@media only screen
and (min-width:576px)
and (max-width:767px)
{
.slider-height {
min-height: 600px
}
}

@media (max-
width:575px) {
.slider-height {
min-height: 640px
}
}
```

For the hero-overly class you have to use a relative position and a z-index *value* of 1.

You also need to use the before attribute. This will be the actual overlay of the image.

Add an absolute position, an empty content, a dark but slightly transparent background-color and 100% as a *value* for the width and height *properties*.

```
.hero-overly {
  position: relative;
  z-index: 1;
}

.hero-overly::before
{
  position: absolute;
  content: "";
  background-color:
  rgba(0, 1, 2, .4);
  width: 100%;
  height: 100%;
}
```

Center the text and set the styling for the headlines. You will center the text with the class "header_caption".

```
.header_caption {
  text-align: center;
}
```

You also need to add the right padding for small screen devices:

```
@media (max-
width:575px) {
```

```
.slider-area
.header_caption {
  padding-top: 100px;
}
}
```

For the <h1> *tag* add a big font size, a bold font weight, a white color, 1.3px as a line height and a bottom margin of 13px.

```
.slider-area
.header_caption h1 {
  font-size: 78px;
  font-weight: 700;
  color: #fff;
  line-height: 1.3;
  margin-bottom:
  13px;
}
```

The *declarations* above also need to be adjusted for different screen sizes:

```
@media only screen and
(min-width:992px) and
(max-width:1199px) {
.slider-area
.header_caption h1 {
  font-size: 60px;
  line-height: 1.2;
}
}

@media only screen
and (min-width:768px)
and (max-width:991px)
{
.slider-area
.header_caption h1 {
  font-size: 50px;
  line-height: 1.2;
}
}

@media only screen
and (min-width:576px)
and (max-width:767px)
{
.slider-area
.header_caption h1 {
  font-size: 51px;
  line-height: 1.2;
  margin-bottom:
  20px;
}
}

@media (max-
width:575px) {
.slider-area
.header_caption h1 {
  font-size: 35px;
  line-height: 1.2;
  margin-bottom:
  20px;
}
}
```

Last but not least you will have to change the span styling. Use the default theme color, give it a big font size set the line-height to 1.2px, add a bold font-weight and a bottom margin of 30px. Additionally set "Sacramento" as the font family. If this font cannott load use cursive as a fallback. Also set the display *property* to block.

```
.slider-area
.header_caption  span
{
  color:  var(--main-
  color);
  font-size: 60px;
  line-height: 1.2;
  font-weight: 400;
  margin-bottom:
  30px;
  font-family:
  Sacramento,
  cursive;
  display:block;
}

@media          (max-
width:575px) {
.slider-area
.header_caption   span
{
  margin-bottom:
  30px;
  font-size: 56px;
}
}
```

YOUR HTML CODE

```
<main>

  <section class="slider-area hero-overly">

    <div class="hero-overly slider-height d-
    flex align-items-center">
      <div class="container">
        <div class="row justify-content-
        center">
          <div class="col-xl-8 col-lg-9">
            <div class="header_caption">
              <span>Welcome</span>
              <h1>Learn HTML & CSS</h1>
            </div>
          </div>
        </div>
      </div>
    </div>

  </section>
```

YOUR CSS CODE

```
/*------------------Slider----------------
-*/

.slider-area {
  background-image: url(imgs/wallpaper.jpg);
  background-size: cover;
  background-repeat: no-repeat;
}

.slider-height {
  min-height: 890px;
  background-repeat: no-repeat;
  background-position: center center;
  background-size: cover;
}

@media only screen and (min-width:992px) and
(max-width:1199px) {
.slider-height {
  min-height: 680px;
}
}

@media only screen and (min-width:768px) and
(max-width:991px) {
.slider-height {
  min-height: 600px;
}
}
```

```
@media only screen and (min-width:576px) and
(max-width:767px) {
.slider-height {
  min-height: 600px;
}
}

@media (max-width:575px) {
.slider-height {
  min-height: 640px;
}
}

.hero-overly {
  position: relative;
  z-index: 1;
}

.hero-overly::before {
  position: absolute;
  content: "";
  background-color: rgba(0, 1, 2, .4);
  width: 100%;
  height: 100%;
}

.header_caption {
  text-align: center;
}

@media (max-width:575px) {
.slider-area .header_caption {
  padding-top: 100px;
}
```

```
}

@media only screen and (min-width:992px) and
(max-width:1199px) {
.slider-area .header_caption h1 {
  font-size: 60px;
  line-height: 1.2;
}
}

@media only screen and (min-width:768px) and
(max-width:991px) {
.slider-area .header_caption h1 {
  font-size: 50px;
  line-height: 1.2;
}
}

@media only screen and (min-width:576px) and
(max-width:767px) {
.slider-area .header_caption h1 {
  font-size: 51px;
  line-height: 1.2;
  margin-bottom: 20px;
}
}

@media (max-width:575px) {
.slider-area .header_caption h1 {
  font-size: 35px;
  line-height: 1.2;
  margin-bottom: 20px;
}
}
```

```
.slider-area .header_caption span {
  color: var(--main-color);
  font-size: 60px;
  line-height: 1.2;
  font-weight: 400;
  margin-bottom: 30px;
  font-family: Sacramento, cursive;
  display: block;
}

@media (max-width:575px) {
.slider-area .header_caption span {
  margin-bottom: 30px;
  font-size: 56px;
}
}

/*-------------------End Slider-------------
----*/
```

PHOTO SECTION

Let's dive right into your next section. This section will be a kind of library for your pictures. In your <main> *tag* create a second section with the id "section_photos". you will use the id to link this section to your *header* links. As you click on "photos" it should automatically bring you to this section.

To make your browser scroll smoothly to the section add this line at the top of your *CSS* sheet:

```
html {
  -webkit-scroll-
  behavior: smooth;
  scroll-behavior:
  smooth;
}
```

In your 'index.html' file create a division inside of your new section. Class it as "row align-items-strech".

Inside of this division you will add all the images.

The following code must be copied as often as you want pictures on your site. On the demo site there are 12 pictures.

```
<div class="col-6
col-md-6 col-lg-4"
data-aos="fade-up">

<a href="imgs/1.jpg"
class="d-block photo-
item" data-
fancybox="gallery">

<img src="imgs/1.jpg"
alt="Image"
class="img-fluid">

</a>
</div>
```

Note for every image you embed, change the *href* and *src* paths to your image links.

Also add the "align-items-strech" class and change the margin to 0.

Use the "col-6" class and set the padding to 0.

Then use the width *property* and set it to 100%. Set the height to 300px, and the margin bottom to 5px.

Now add a *property* called *object-fit* and set it to cover. This will have the same effect as the *declaration*: "background-size: cover" with the only difference that this *property* uses a <img> *tag* instead of a background image. It simply fills the space you gave the *container*.

```
.align-items-stretch {
  margin: 0;
}

.col-6 {
padding: 0;
}

.img-fluid {
  width: 100%;
  object-fit: cover;
  height: 300px;
  margin-bottom: 5px;
  box-sizing: border-
  box;
  }

  @media only screen
  and (max-
  width:575px) {
  .img-fluid {
  height: 200px;
  }
```

YOUR HTML CODE

```
<section id="section-photos">

  <div class="row align-items-stretch">

    <div class="col-6 col-md-6 col-lg-4"
    data-aos="fade-up"><a href="imgs/1.jpg"
    class="d-block photo-item" data-
    fancybox="gallery"><img src="imgs/1.jpg"
    alt="Image" class="img-fluid"></a></div>

    <div class="col-6 col-md-6 col-lg-4"
    data-aos="fade-up" data-aos-delay="100">
    <a href="imgs/2.jpg" class="d-block
    photo-item" data-fancybox="gallery">
    <img src="imgs/2.jpg" alt="Image"
    class="img-fluid"></a></div>

    <div class="col-6 col-md-6 col-lg-4"
    data-aos="fade-up" data-aos-delay="200">
    <a href="imgs/3.jpg" class="d-block
    photo-item" data-fancybox="gallery">
    <img src="imgs/3.jpg" alt="Image"
    class="img-fluid"></a></div>

    <div class="col-6 col-md-6 col-lg-4"
    data-aos="fade-up"> <a href="imgs/4.jpg"
    class="d-block photo-item" data-
    fancybox="gallery"> <img
    src="imgs/4.jpg" alt="Image" class="img-
    fluid"></a></div>
```

YOUR CSS CODE

```
/*------------Pictures Adjustment-----------
-*/

.align-items-stretch {
  margin: 0;
}

.col-6 {
  padding: 0;
}

.img-fluid {
  width: 100%;
  object-fit: cover;
  height: 300px;
  margin-bottom: 5px;
  box-sizing: border-box;
}

@media only screen and (max-width:575px) {
.img-fluid {
  height: 200px;
}
}

/*----------End Pictures Adjustment---------
-*/
```

BLOG AREA

Create a section and add the classes "home-blog-area" and "section-padding" and use the id "blog-section". Then create an overall *Bootstrap container* and two rows. You will use the first row to add the heading and the second to add the blog posts. In the first one add a division with the class "col-lg-12". Inside of it add a division with the class "section-title text-center". Then add a span and an <h2> *tag*.

```
<section class="home-blog-area section-padding" id="blog-section">

<div class="container">

<div class="row">

<div class="col-lg-12">

<div class="section-tittle text-center">
<span>My blog</span>
<h2>Newest</h2>

</div>
</div>

<div class="row">
</div>
</div>

</section>
```

In the second row create a division with the classes "col-xl-4 col-lg-4 col-md-6 col-sm-6". Now add a division with the class "blog post" and inside of it create a division with the class "blog-img". Add the <img> *tag* with the source of your image and an alt *attribute*.

Under the "blog-img" box there is a second section with the class "blog-caption", which will serve as a *container* for your headlines. Use the <h3> *tag* and create a link in it. Add your headline for the blog post. Add a <p> *tag* below the <h3> *tag* and write your subheading.

```
<div class="col-xl-4
```

```
col-lg-4 col-md-6
col-sm-6">

<img
src="imgs/img2.jpg"
alt=""></div>

<div class="blog-
caption">

<h3><a
href="blog.html">My
first blog post</a>
</h3>

<p>September 1, 1998
by Robin</p>

</div>
</div>
</div>
```

Repeat this step until you have three blog posts.

Now you will have to change the *CSS*.

For the class "blog-img" set the overflow to hidden. Add a bottom margin of 19px and create rounded corners.

Note: the *declaration* overflow hidden will simply hide all the content outside of the margins of your division. In this particular case it will hide the corners of your images.

For the pictures of the class "blog-img" add a width of 100%, a transition of "all .6s ease-out 0" and add the *declaration* "transform: scale(1)".

You will not see the changes immediately for that last *declaration*, but as you hover of the image you will change the transform *property* to "scale(1.1)". It will create an inner zoom effect.

Add the hover effect.

```
.blog-img {
  overflow: hidden;
  margin-bottom:
  19px;
  border-radius:
  12px;
}

.blog-img img {
  width: 100%;
  transform:
  scale(1);
  transition: all .6s
  ease-out 0s;
```

```
}

.blog-post:hover
.blog-img img {
  transform:
  scale(1.1);
}
```

Let's now change the styling of the blog posts' titles:

```
.blog-caption h3 {
  padding-right:
  48px;
  margin-bottom:
  17px;
}

@media only screen
and (min-width:768px)
and (max-width:991px)
{
  .blog-caption h3 {
  padding-right: 0;
}
}

@media only screen
and (min-width:576px)
and (max-width:767px)
{
.blog-caption h3 {
  padding-right: 0;
}
}

@media (max-
width:575px) {
  .blog-caption h3 {
  padding-right: 0;
}
}

.blog-caption h3 a {
  color: #1c1930;
  font-weight: 700;
  font-size: 25px;
}

.blog-caption p {
  color: #57667e;
}
```

Change the overall title of your blog section.

For the class "section-title" simply add a margin bottom and change it for small screen devices.

```
.section-tittle {
  margin-bottom:
  70px;
}

@media (max-
width:575px) {
.section-tittle {
  margin-bottom: 50px
}
}

@media only screen and
(min-width:576px) and
```

```
(max-width:767px) {
.section-tittle {
    margin-bottom:
    50px;
  }
}
```

Also change the sub-headline with the following attributes:

```
.section-tittle span
{
  font-size: 30px;
  font-weight: 700;
  margin-bottom:
  22px;
  color:  var(--main-
  color);
  display: inline-
  block;
  font-family:
  Sacramento,
  cursive;
}

.section-tittle h2 {
  font-size: 50px;
  display: block;
  color: #1c1930;
  font-weight: 600;
}

@media  only  screen
and  (min-width:576px)
and  (max-width:767px)
{
.section-tittle h2 {
  font-size: 31px;
   text-align: center;
}
}

@media          (max-
width:575px) {
.section-tittle h2 {
   text-align: center;
   font-size: 31px;
}
}
```

With the last lines you changed the font, size, boldness, margin and you added the default color to you headline.

In addition, you have changed the size, display *attribute*, color and bold font in the subheading.

When you created your *HTML* code, you added a class called "section-padding". With the following lines you can adapt it to the different screen sizes of your website.

```
.section-padding {
  padding-top: 195px;
  padding-bottom:
  140px;
}
```

```
@media only screen
and (min-
width:1200px) and
(max-width:1600px) {
.section-padding {
   padding-top: 195px;
   padding-bottom:
   140px;
}
}

@media only screen
and (min-width:992px)
and (max-
width:1199px) {
.section-padding {
   padding-top: 150px;
   padding-bottom:
   90px;
}
}

@media only screen
and (min-width:768px)
and
(max-width:991px) {
.section-padding {
   padding-top: 100px;
   padding-bottom:
   40px;
}
}

@media only screen
and (min-width:576px)
and (max-width:767px)
{
.section-padding {
   padding-top: 65px;

@media only screen
and (min-width:576px)
and (max-width:767px)
{
.section-padding {
   padding-top: 65px;
   padding-bottom:
   10px;
}
}

@media (max-
width:575px) {
.section-padding {
   padding-top: 65px;
   padding-bottom:
   10px;
}
}
```

YOUR HTML CODE

```
<section class="home-blog-area section-
padding" id="blog-section">
  <div class="container">

    <div class="row">
      <div class="col-lg-12">
        <div class="section-tittle text-
        center">
          <span>My blog</span>
          <h2>Newest</h2>
        </div>
      </div>
    </div>

    <div class="row">

      <div class="col-xl-4 col-lg-4 col-md-6
      col-sm-6">
        <div class="blog-post">
          <div class="blog-img"> <img
          src="imgs/img2.jpg" alt=""></div>
            <div class="blog-caption">
              <h3><a href="blog.html">My
              first blog post</a></h3>
              <p>September 1, 1998 by
              Robin</p>
            </div>
          </div>
        </div>
```

```
        <div class="col-xl-4 col-lg-4 col-md-6
        col-sm-6">
          <div class="blog-post">
            <div class="blog-img"> <img
            src="imgs/img3.jpg" alt=""></div
            <div class="blog-caption">
              <h3><a href="blog.html">My
              second blog post</a></h3>
              <p>August 1, 20222 by Robin</p
            </div>
          </div>
        </div>

        <div class="col-xl-4 col-lg-4 col-md-6
        col-sm-6">
          <div class="blog-post">
            <div class="blog-img"> <img
            src="imgs/img4.jpg" alt=""></div>
            <div class="blog-caption">
              <h3><a href="blog.html">My
              third blog post</a></h3>
              <p>November 6, 3021 by
              Robin</p>
            </div>
          </div>
        </div>
      </div>
    </div>
  </section>
```

YOUR CSS CODE

```
/*-----------------Blog Section-----------
--*/

.blog-img {
  overflow: hidden;
  margin-bottom: 19px;
  border-radius: 12px;
}

.blog-img img {
  width: 100%;
  transform: scale(1);
  transition: all .6s ease-out 0s;
}

.blog-post:hover .blog-img img {
  transform: scale(1.1);
}

.blog-caption h3 {
  padding-right: 48px;
  margin-bottom: 17px;
}

@media only screen and (min-width:768px)
and (max-width:991px) {
.blog-caption h3 {
  padding-right: 0;
}
}
```

```
@media only screen and (min-width:576px)
and (max-width:767px) {
.blog-caption h3 {
  padding-right: 0;
}
}

@media (max-width:575px) {
.blog-caption h3 {
  padding-right: 0;
}
}

.blog-caption h3 a {
  color: #1c1930;
  font-weight: 700;
  font-size: 25px;
}

.blog-caption p {
  color: #57667e;
}

.section-tittle {
  margin-bottom: 70px;
}

@media (max-width:575px) {
.section-tittle {
  margin-bottom: 50px;
}
}
```

```
@media only screen and (min-width:576px)
and (max-width:767px) {
.section-tittle {
  margin-bottom: 50px;
}
}

.section-tittle span {
  font-size: 30px;
  font-weight: 700;
  margin-bottom: 22px;
  color: var(--main-color);
  display: inline-block;
  font-family: Sacramento, cursive;
}

.section-tittle h2 {
  font-size: 50px;
  display: block;
  color: #1c1930;
  font-weight: 600;
}

@media only screen and (min-width:576px)
and (max-width:767px) {
.section-tittle h2 {
  font-size: 31px;
  text-align: center;
}
}

@media (max-width:575px) {
```

```
.section-tittle h2 {
  text-align: center;
  font-size: 31px;
}
}

.section-padding {
  padding-top: 195px;
  padding-bottom: 140px;
}

@media only screen and (min-width:1200px)
and (max-width:1600px) {
.section-padding {
  padding-top: 195px;
  padding-bottom: 140px;
}
}

@media only screen and (min-width:992px)
and (max-width:1199px) {
.section-padding {
  padding-top: 150px;
  padding-bottom: 90px;
}
}

@media only screen and (min-width:768px)
and (max-width:991px) {
.section-padding {
  padding-top: 100px;
  padding-bottom: 40px;
}
}
```

```
@media only screen and (min-width:576px)
and (max-width:767px) {
.section-padding {
  padding-top: 65px;
  padding-bottom: 10px;
}
}

@media (max-width:575px) {
.section-padding {
  padding-top: 65px;
  padding-bottom: 10px;
}
}

/*--------------End Blog Section-----------
--*/
```

VIDEO

Create a division in your last section. Give it a 'history-video-area' class and the 'about-section' Id.

In it, create a *container*, a row and a column classified as "col-lg-6". This will be the area of the video image. Create an additional subdivision called "video-bg" and add an image and a subdivision. Implement the source of your image in the <img> *tag* and add the class "video-icon" to the second subdivision.

Create a link with the class "btn-icon" and the *attribute* href="" of the video you want to include. You might want to add the *attribute* "target="blank"" which opens your links in a new *tab*. Within your link, add the span *attribute* and the fontawesome class "fa-play".

```
<section
class="history-video-
area" id="about-
section">

<div
class="container">

<div class="row">

<div class="col-lg-
6">

<div class="video-
bg">

<img
src="imgs/img1.jpg"
alt="">

<div    class="video-
icon">
<a    class="btn-icon"
href="https://www.you
tube.com/watch?
v=By_fjTnQ0hg"
tabindex="0"
target="_blank">

<span  class="fa  fa-
play"></span>

</a>
</div>
</div>
</div>
```

Now underneath your "col-lg-6" class create a

second column with the same name. Add a division "video-history-cap" and include an <h3> title and a <p> text.

Under your <p> *tag* add a link with the class "btn". This will be the button of the about us section.

In your *CSS* add the class "history-video-area" and change the top and bottom padding to 100px so that there is space between the sections.

Change the "video-bg" *container* to "z-index": 1" so it appears above the text, and change its position to "relative".

Within the same class change the padding for the small and middle screen devices.

```
.history-video-area {
  padding: 100px 0;
}

.video-bg {
  position: relative;
  z-index: 1;
}

@media only screen
and (min-width:768px)
and (max-width:991px)
{
.video-bg {
  margin-bottom:
  80px;
}
}

@media only screen
and (min-width:576px)
and (max-width:767px)
{
.video-bg {
  margin-bottom:
  50px;
}
}

@media              (max-
width:767px) {
.video-bg {
  margin-bottom:
  50px;
}
}
```

Also change the image to 100% of the column width, set the icon *container* to position absolute and set the left and right *attribute* to 0 so it gets centered horizontally. Also set the top *attribute* to 50% and the text alignment to center.

Finally, use the transform "translateY(50%)" *attribute*. This *value* in combination with the top 50% will center your button vertically.

```
.video-bg img {
  width: 100%;
}

.video-icon {
  position: absolute;
  left: 0;
  right: 0;
  top: 50%;
  text-align: center;
  transform:
  translateY(-50%);
}
```

Next change the actual button style. On the demo page, the background is set to white and the color of the icon is set to the default theme color you have defined at the beginning.

Set the width and the height of the link to 80px and change the display *attribute* to inline-block, the line-height to 80px, so the icon gets centered vertically, and round the corners. Finally, add a relative position.

```
.btn-icon {
  background: #fff;
  color: var(--main-
  color);
  width: 80px;
  height: 80px;
  display: inline-
  block;
  text-align: center;
  line-height: 80px;
  border-radius: 50%;
  border-radius: 50%;
  position: relative;
}
```

Now add a slight animation around the link. To do so add a before *pseudo-element* and set the content to empty. Set the position to absolute and the display *property* to inline-block. Also add the *properties* top, right, bottom, left and give them a *value* of -2px.

Notice, if you came to set the top, right, bottom, left *properties* to *values* like "-10px" or "-50px" it would enlarge your animation.

Set the border-radius to inherit. This will adjust the element to its *container*.

Add a 1px solid border with your main color.

Finally set the Animation *property* to "VidAnim 2s cubic-bezier(0.23, 1, .32, 1) both infinite". "VidAnim" is the name of the animation that lasts for 2 seconds, "cubic-bezier" is a special animation type that you can customize as needed, and the *value* "both" will cause your element to follow the animation guidelines from 0% to 100% and vice versa from 100% to 0%. The *value* "infinite" allows your element to repeat the animation infinitely.

Now use *keyframes* to define now the animation:

```
@keyframes VidAnim {
0% {
  border-width: 4px;
  -webkit-transform:
  scale(1);
  transform:
  scale(1);
}

50% {
  border-width: 1px;
  -webkit-transform:
  scale(1.5);
  transform:
  scale(1.5);
}

80% {
  border-width: 1px;
  -webkit-transform:
  scale(1.9);
  transform:
  scale(1.9);
}

100% {
  opacity: 0;
}
}
```

Repeat this step with the @-webkit-keyframes *attribute* to make it available to all browsers.

Add the hover *pseudo-class* for the icon *container*:

```
.btn-icon:hover {
  background:
  #234249;
  color: #fff;
}
```

Change the style of the text and of the video section:

```
.video-history-text {
  background:
  #f4efe6;
```

```
60px 161px;
  position: relative;
  margin-left:
  -130px;
  margin-top: -62px;
  z-index: 0;
}
```

Adjust the margins and the paddings for middle and small screen devices:

```
@media only screen
and (min-width:992px)
and (max-
width:1199px) {

.video-history-text {
  padding: 42px 34px
  34px 131px;
  margin-left:
  -106px;
  margin-top: -41px;
}
}

@media (max-
width:767px) {
.video-history-text {
  margin-left: 0;
  padding: 50px 16px;
  margin-top: -30px;
}
}

@media only screen
and (min-width:576px)
and (max-width:767px)
{
.video-history-text {
  margin-left: 0;
  padding: 50px 16px;
  margin-top: -30px;
}
}

@media only screen
and (min-width:576px)
and (max-width:767px)
{
.video-history-text {
  margin-left: 0;
  padding: 50px 20px
  50px 25px;
  margin-top: -46px;
}
}

@media only screen
and (min-width:768px)
and (max-width:991px)
{
.video-history-text {
  margin-left: 0;
  padding: 50px 48px;
  margin-left: 0;
  padding: 50px 48px
  50px 59px;
}
}
```

Next change the color, the font-size, font-weight, line-height and margin of your <h3> title.

```
.video-history-text h3
{
   color: #161922;
   font-size: 60px;
   font-weight: 600;
   line-height: 1.1;
   margin-bottom:
   28px;
}

@media only screen and
(min-width:992px) and
(max-width:1199px) {
.video-history-text h3
{
   margin-bottom:
   18px;
}
}

@media (max-
width:767px) {
.video-history-text h3
{
   font-size: 42px;
}
}
```

You will also need to change the the actual text style:

```
.video-history-text p
{
  color: #161922;
  font-size: 16px;
  margin-bottom:
  42px;
}

@media only screen and
(min-width:992px) and
(max-width:1199px) {
.video-history-text p
{
margin-bottom: 28px;
}
}
```

Last but not least edit the styling of the button under your text;

```
.btn {
  background: var(--
  main-color);
  border-radius:
  30px;
  -moz-user-select:
  none;
  text-transform:
  uppercase;
  font-family:
  "Sulphur Point",
  sans-serif;
  color: #fff;
  display: inline-
  block;
  font-size: 14px;
  font-weight: 500;
  letter-spacing:
  1px;
  line-height: 0;
  padding: 27px 44px;
  cursor: pointer;
  position: relative;
}
```

YOUR HTML CODE

```
<section class="history-video-area section-
padding" id="about-section">

  <div class="container">
    <div class="row">

      <div class="col-lg-6">
        <div class="video-bg">
          <img src="imgs/img1.jpg" alt="">
          <div class="video-icon">
            <a class="btn-icon"
            href="https://www.youtube.com/w
            atch?v=By_fjTnQ0hg"
            tabindex="0" target="_blank">
              <span class="fa fa-play">
              </span>
            </a>
          </div>
        </div>
      </div>

      <div class="col-lg-6">
        <div class="video-history-text">
          <h3>My Story</h3>
          <p>Lorem Ipsum ... </p>
          <a href="about.html"
          class="btn">About Us</a
        </div>
      </div>
    </div>
  </div>

</section>
```

YOUR CSS CODE

```
/*---------------Video Section--------------
-*/


.history-video-area {
  padding: 100px 0;
}

.video-bg {
  position: relative;
  z-index: 1;
}

@media only screen and (min-width:768px) and
(max-width:991px) {
.video-bg {
  margin-bottom: 80px;
}
}

@media only screen and (min-width:576px) and
(max-width:767px) {
.video-bg {
  margin-bottom: 50px;
}
}

@media (max-width:767px) {
.video-bg {
  margin-bottom: 50px;
}
}
```

```
.video-bg img {
  width: 100%;
}

.video-icon {
  position: absolute;
  left: 0;
  right: 0;
  top: 50%;
  text-align: center;
  transform: translateY(-50%);
}

.btn-icon {
  background: #fff;
  color: var(--main-color);
  width: 80px;
  height: 80px;
  display: inline-block;
  text-align: center;
  line-height: 80px;
  border-radius: 50%;
  position: relative;
}

.btn-icon::before {
  content: '';
  display: inline-block;
  position: absolute;
  top: -2px;
  left: -2px;
  bottom: -2px;
  right: -2px;
  border-radius: inherit;
```

```
  border: 1px solid var(--main-color);
  -webkit-animation: VidAnim 2s cubic-
  bezier(0.23, 1, .32, 1) both infinite;
  animation: VidAnim 2s cubic-bezier(0.23,
  1, .32, 1) both infinite;
}

@-webkit-keyframes VidAnim {
0% {
  border-width: 4px;
  -webkit-transform: scale(1);
  transform: scale(1);
}

50% {
  border-width: 1px;
  -webkit-transform: scale(1.5);
  transform: scale(1.5);
}

80% {
  border-width: 1px;
  -webkit-transform: scale(1.9);
  transform: scale(1.9);
}

100% {
  opacity: 0;
}
}

@keyframes VidAnim {
0% {
  border-width: 4px;
```

```
    -webkit-transform: scale(1);
    transform: scale(1);
  }

  50% {
    border-width: 1px;
    -webkit-transform: scale(1.5);
    transform: scale(1.5);
  }

  80% {
    border-width: 1px;
    -webkit-transform: scale(1.9);
    transform: scale(1.9);
  }

  100% {
    opacity: 0;
  }
  }

  .btn-icon:hover {
    background: #234249;
    color: #fff;
  }

  .video-history-text {
    background: #f4efe6;
    padding: 60px 70px 60px 161px;
    position: relative;
    margin-left: -130px;
    margin-top: -62px;
    z-index: 0;
  }
```

```
@media only screen and (min-width:992px)
and (max-width:1199px) {
.video-history-text {
   padding: 42px 34px 34px 131px;
   margin-left: -106px;
   margin-top: -41px;
}
}

@media (max-width:767px) {
.video-history-text {
   margin-left: 0;
   padding: 50px 16px;
   margin-top: -30px;
}
}

@media only screen and (min-width:576px)
and (max-width:767px) {
.video-history-text {
   margin-left: 0;
   padding: 50px 20px 50px 25px;
   margin-top: -46px;
}
}

@media only screen and (min-width:768px)
and (max-width:991px) {
.video-history-text {
   margin-left: 0;
   padding: 50px 48px 50px 59px;
}
}
```

```
.video-history-text {
  margin-left: 0;
  padding: 50px 48px 50px 59px;
}
}

.video-history-text h3 {
  color: #161922;
  font-size: 60px;
  font-weight: 600;
  line-height: 1.1;
  margin-bottom: 28px;
}

@media only screen and (min-width:992px)
and (max-width:1199px) {
.video-history-text h3 {
  margin-bottom: 18px;
}
}

@media (max-width:767px) {
.video-history-text h3 {
  font-size: 42px;
}
}

@media only screen and (min-width:576px)
and (max-width:767px) {
.video-history-text h3 {
  font-size: 42px;
}
}
```

```
.video-history-text p {
  color: #161922;
  font-size: 16px;
  margin-bottom: 42px;
}

@media only screen and (min-width:992px)
and (max-width:1199px) {
.video-history-text p {
  margin-bottom: 28px;
}
}


.btn {
  background: var(--main-color);
  border-radius: 30px;
  -moz-user-select: none;
  text-transform: uppercase;
  font-family: "Sulphur Point", sans-serif;
  color: #fff;
  display: inline-block;
  font-size: 14px;
  font-weight: 500;
  letter-spacing: 1px;
  line-height: 0;
  padding: 27px 44px;
  cursor: pointer;
  position: relative;
}
```

FOOTER

Congratulations! At this point your site should already look pretty good! You just need to add a footer to make it complete.

Create the <footer> *tag* and insert two divisions into each other with the classes "footer-area" and the second with the class "footer-copy-right".

```
<footer>

<div class="footer-
area">

<div class="footer-
copy-right">

</div>

</div>

</footer>
```

Inside the last one create a paragraph with the text: "Copyright ©". Then add a script *tag* displaying the current year your are in.

Finish your statement with "All rights reserved".

```
<p> Copyright &copy;

<script>
document.write(new
Date().getFullYear())
;
</script>

All rights reserved
</p>
```

In your *CSS* give the overall "footer-area" *container* a 100% width and a dark background-color.

For your text use a lighter color, a bold font weight, a 16px font size and a top and bottom padding of 32px. Also add a top and bottom margin of 0 and center the text alignment:

```
.footer-area {
  width: 100%;
  background:
  #030f23;
}

.footer-copy-right p
{
   color: #8ba4b1;
```

```
    font-weight: 300;
    font-size: 16px;
    padding: 32px 0;
    margin: 0 auto;
    text-align: center;
}


@media (max-width:575px) {
.footer-copy-right p {
   padding: 30px 0 30px 0px;
   font-size: 12px;
}
}
```

You have successfully built your website! If you like, you can add a loading screen, which I will show you on the next pages. If you don't want to do that, just go to the next chapter where you will upload your website.

YOUR HTML CODE

```
<footer>

  <div class="footer-area">
    <div class="footer-copy-right">

      <p> Copyright &copy;

      <script>
        document.write(new
        Date().getFullYear());
      </script>

      All rights reserved
      </p>

    </div>
  </div>

</footer>
```

YOUR CSS CODE

```
.footer-area {
  width: 100%;
  background: #030f23;
}

.footer-copy-right p {
  color: #8ba4b1;
  font-weight: 300;
  font-size: 16px;
  padding: 32px 0;
  margin: 0 auto;
  text-align: center;
}

.footer-area {
  width: 100%;
  background: #030f23;
}

.footer-copy-right p {
  color: #8ba4b1;
  font-weight: 300;
  font-size: 16px;
  padding: 32px 0;
  margin: 0 auto;
  text-align: center;
}

@media (max-width:575px) {
.footer-copy-right p {
  padding: 30px 0 30px 0px;
  font-size: 12px;
}
}
```

THE PRELOADER

Over your *header*, add a division with the class "preloader". Insert two subdivisions called "pre-loader-circle" and "pre-loader-text". Inside of the preloader text add the name you want to appear on your loading screen.

```
<div
class="preloader">

<div
class="preloader-
circle"></div>

<div
class="preloader-
text">

Loading

</div>
</div>
```

For the *CSS* part simply set the position of the preloader to fixed, add a light background color, set the width and the height to 100% so it takes up the entire screen and set the z-index to "999999" to be sure it is the first element the user sees.

```
.preloader {
  position: fixed;
  background-color:
  #f7f7f7;
  width: 100%;
  height: 100%;
  z-index: 999999;
}
```

Also edit the loading animation. For the class "preloader-circle" add a width and a height of 100px. Set the border style to "1px solid" and only add the default theme color to the top border. Then create rounded corners, use a white background, set the position to absolute and the top, right, bottom, left *attributes* to 0, with a margin "auto". Additionally, use a box shadow and an animation.

```
.preloader-circle {
  width: 100px;
  height: 100px;
  border-style:
```

```
    solid;
    border-width: 1px;
    border-color: var(-
    -main-color)
    transparent
    transparent;
    border-radius: 50%;
    background: #fff;
    position: absolute;
    load 2000ms
    infinite ease;
    animation: load
    2000ms infinite
    ease;
}
```

Change the style of the inner text of your loading screen.

Add an absolute position, a top *attribute* of 50%, a transform translateY of "50%", sans-serif as the font and an inline-block display *attribute*. Also set the left and right *properties* to 0 and set the text alignment to center.

```
.preloader-text {
    position: absolute;
    top: 50%;
    transform:
    translateY(-50%);
    left: 0;
    right: 0;
    text-align: center;
    display: inline-
    block;
    font-family:  sans-
    serif;
}
```

Create the animation by adding two percentages. The first is 0% and the second 100%. For the first one include the transform *property* with the transform rotate *value* of 0 degrees. For the second one use the *value* 360 degrees.

```
@-webkit-keyframes
load {
0% {
    -webkit-transform:
    rotate(0deg);
    transform:
    rotate(0deg);
}

100% {
    -webkit-transform:
    rotate(360deg);
    transform:
    rotate(360deg);
}
}

@keyframes load {
```

```
0% {
  -webkit-transform:
  rotate(0deg);
  transform:
  rotate(0deg);
}

100% {
  -webkit-transform:
  rotate(360deg);
  transform:
  rotate(360deg);
}
}
```

Your preloader is almost finished. Just add some JavaScript to it, so it fades away once your site is loaded:

```
/* 1. Proloder */
e(window).on("load",
function () {
  e(".preloader").del
  ay(450).fadeOut("sl
  ow")
});
```

YOUR HTML CODE

```
<div class="preloader">

  <div class="preloader-circle"></div>
  <div class="preloader-text">
    Robin
  </div>

</div>
```

YOUR JAVASCRIPT CODE

```
/* 1. Proloder */

e(window).on("load", function () {
  e(".preloader").delay(450).fadeOut("slow"
  )
});
```

YOUR CSS CODE

```
.preloader {
  position: fixed;
  background-color: #f7f7f7;
  width: 100%;
  height: 100%;
  z-index: 999999;
}

.preloader-circle {
  width: 100px;
  height: 100px;
  border-style: solid;
  border-width: 1px;
  border-color: var(--main-color)
  transparent transparent;
  border-radius: 50%;
  background: #fff;
  position: absolute;
  left: 0;
  right: 0;
  top: 0;
  bottom: 0;
  margin: auto;
  -webkit-box-shadow: 0 1px 5px 0 rgba(35,
  181, 185, .15);
  box-shadow: 0 1px 5px 0 rgba(35, 181,
  185, .15);
  -webkit-animation: load 2000ms infinite
  ease;
  animation: load 2000ms infinite ease;
  }
```

```
.preloader-text {
  position: absolute;
  top: 50%;
  transform: translateY(-50%);
  left: 0;
  right: 0;
  text-align: center;
  display: inline-block;
  font-family: sans-serif;
}

@-webkit-keyframes load {
0% {
  -webkit-transform: rotate(0deg);
  transform: rotate(0deg);
}

100% {
  -webkit-transform: rotate(360deg);
  transform: rotate(360deg);
}
}

@keyframes load {
0% {
  -webkit-transform: rotate(0deg);
  transform: rotate(0deg);
}

100% {
  -webkit-transform: rotate(360deg);
  transform: rotate(360deg);
}
```

YOUR WEBSITE GOES ONLINE

7.

HOW TO UPLOAD YOUR SITE?

An upload corresponds to sending data to a remote system such as a server so that the remote system can store a copy of it. When you upload a file, the data goes from your computer to an external server. If you download a file, on the other hand, you get the information from a server.

To upload a website, you need 3 things:

- At first you need a website (which you should have at this point).
- Then you need a domain such as "google.com", "youtube.com" or "bing.com".
- The last thing you need is hosting. Hosting is a server or a computer that is always turned on. Your site will be uploaded to this computer and by typing your domain in the search bar, your PC connects to the server and receives the *HTML* information.

Be warned, you will have to pay money in order to get your site online.

If you are not sure whether you should spend 30$/€ per year on your website, just keep practicing until you feel comfortable.

If you do want to upload your site though here is what you need to do:

Choose a hosting platform. There are lots of hosting companies, but the best ones for getting started are:
- GoDaddy
- OVH
- Bluehost

All hosting platforms have advantages and disadvantages. I don't want to recommend GoDaddy, yet for my use it met the criteria. Note that you have to pay on all platforms and that the fees are similar. Also note that the links are not affiliated.

Go to robinkbr.com /godaddy and choose your domain name. After you got your domain go through the buying process and login to your new account.

Also go to robinkbr.com/ssl to get your own SSL certificate.

SSL stands for Secure Sockets Layer. It is a digital certificate that enables authentication for a website and enables an encrypted connection. SSL-encrypted websites can be accessed via "https" instead of just "http". Note that browsers tend to block "http" websites with messages like "Website not secure".

Once you see the GoDaddy home page click on 'Your Name' > "My Products".

Click on your hosting credit and hit "set up". Select your domain and finish the last set up steps.

As you see the sceen on the image below click on "cPannel Admin"

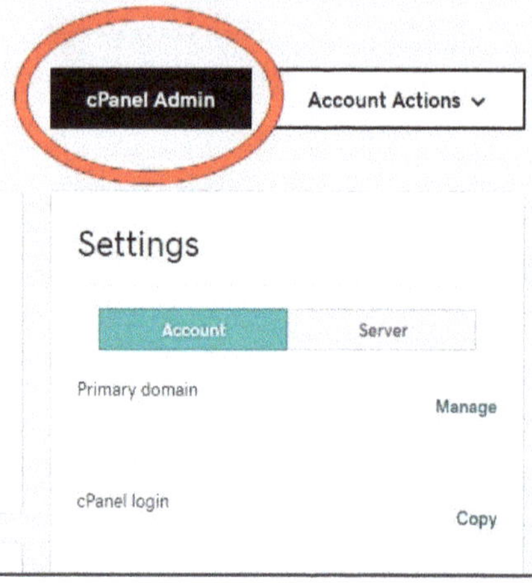

Then click on "file manager":

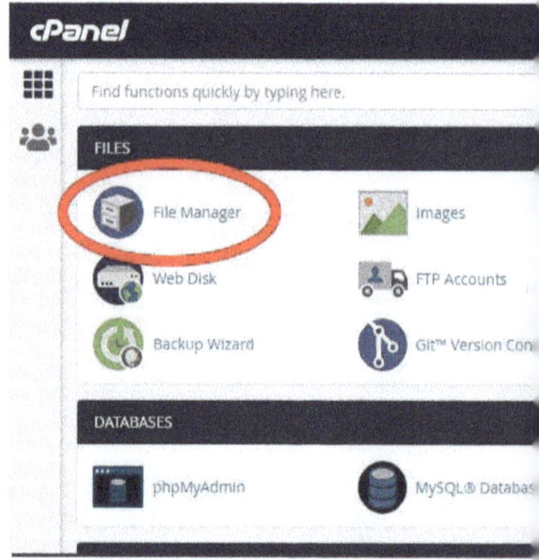

To upload your website, it is easier if you have your documents and folders as a ".zip" file. Go to freetoolonline.com/zipfile.html and drag your files into the site. It is important to drag them, because your folders are not recognized otherwise. Then click on "zip" and "download".

You can also create a ".zip" file by right-clicking on your folder and clicking "Send to" and "Compressed (zipped) folder".

Once finished, go to the "www" directory of your File Manager and upload your ".zip" file.

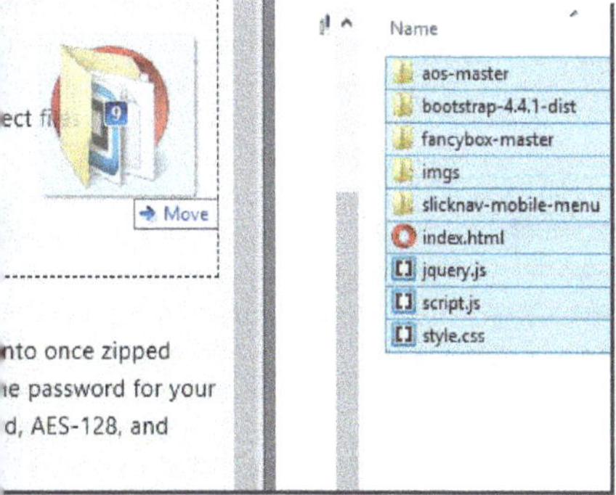

The last step is to extract the file so that browsers can read the actual *HTML* and *CSS* documents.

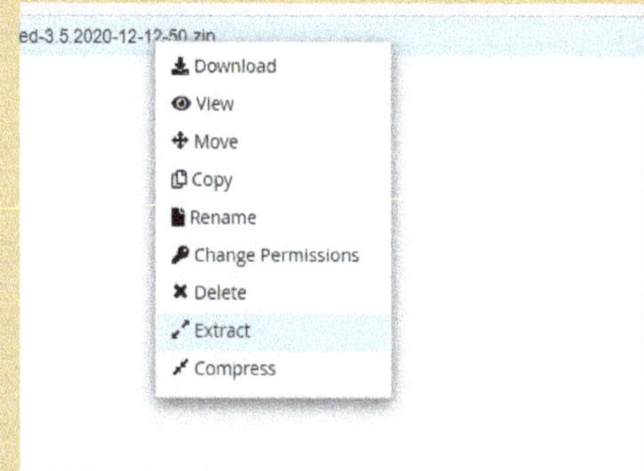

Go to yourdomain.com and enjoy what you created.

Give yourself a pat on the back for having created and uploaded a full *HTML* website!

If this book helped you creating a website, feel free to leave an Amazon review.

Good luck on your future path as a programmer!

CONGRATULATIONS!

YOU'VE SUCCESSFULLY CREATED YOUR FIRST WEBSITE!

<!--comment-->

Comments are not used by browsers. Their only purpose is to help the programmer to keep his/her code clean and to add notes between the lines.

35

<!DOCTYPE HTML>

Information that tells the browser what kind of document to expect.

20

<html>

First *HTML tag* on the Site. It indicates that the coming document is an *HTML* document.

20

<a>

<a> *tags* define hyperlinks. You can either link to external website such as "https://wikipedia.com" or to an internal website such as "your website.com/about"

30

<b>

<b> makes text appear in bold.

28

<base>

The base *tag* is used the *head* of an *HTML* document. It transforms the link <a href="about"> to <a href="yourwebsite/about">

21

<body>

The *body* is the *container* of every *HTML* element you see on the site.

27

 inserts a line break between two text passages. This would be the same as typing "Enter" on a Word document.

29

<button>

The button *tag* defines a clickable button on a website.

37

<div>

A division corresponds a *container* for *HTML* elements. Divisions have no default *CSS properties*, each one must be styles individually via Classes and Ids.

29

<footer>

A <footer> is used as a *container* for the bottom

information of a website. The text "All rights reserved" is usually shown in a footer.

<form>

The <form> *tag* creates an online form. Popular forms include contact or survey forms.

35

<h1>

<h1>, <h2>, <h3>,... <h6> are used to display headlines. They can be used by search engines to rank your content.

27

<head>

The head *tag* is metaphorically speaking the brain of your website. It is used to define the title, keywords and to link external documents.

20

<header>

The is usually the first *tag* inside of the <body>. It is used as a *container* for the top navigation links and for the logo of the site.

33

<hr>

<hr> is used to add a vertival line.

34

href

Href is an *HTML attribute* used to define the URL of a link. It is often used in combination with the <a> *tag*.

<i>

<i> shows text in italics.

28

<iframe>

<iframe> is used to embed documents in a webpage. You can for example embed a YouTube video.

32

<img>

The <img> *tag* is used to link images.

30

<input>

The input field specifies an area in which the user can enter his/her information

36

<label>

A label allows you to classify a specific input field.

36

<li>

Li is the *child* of the <ul> element. It is a list item.

34

<link>

The link *tag* is used to connect your current *HTML* document to an external resource such as a 'style.css' document.

21

<main>

The <main> *tag* is usually the *container* of each section of the website.

33

<meta>

This *tag* provides *metadata* such as the author, descrip-tion, key-words or the viewport of the website.
23

<nav>

The <nav> *tag* is the *container* of the <header> *tag* and is the *container* of the top navigation links.
33

<noscript>

<noscript> provides alternative content for users who have disabled *JavaScript* in their browser.
24

<option>

The <option> *tag* is *the child of the <select> tag. They are used to create dropdown menus.*
36

<p>

<p> stands for paragraph and is used for longer text passages.
28

<script>

You can include the language *JavaScript* directly inside of an *HTML* document.
24

<section>

A section is usually a larger piece of content within the <main> *tag*.
24

<select>

<select> is the *parent* of the <option> *tag*. They are used to create dropdown menus.
36

<span>

<span> is used for small pieces of content withing a *container*. A single word in a paragraph could be a <span>.
34

<strike>

The <strike> *tag* crosses text passages.
29

<style>

<style> *tags* are used to embed the programming language *CSS* within an *HTML* document.
21

<textarea>

It is often used as comment section on *HTML* forms.
37

<title>

The title is displayed in the *tab* of your browser. Search engines also use the title to rank your website.
21

<u>

The <u> *tag* creates underlined text.
28

<ul>

<ul> creates unordered list. It is the *parent* of the <li> *tag*. 34

<video>

The <video> *tag* links a video to a website. It supports .mp4, .ogg and .WebM files. You can also specify the beginning, the end and the loop the video. 31

Quick Reference to

{ CSS }

align-items:

The "align-items" *property* sets the vertical alignment of a flex item.

70

background:

The background *property* defines background color, image, position, attachment, size of an element.

47

border:

The border *property* allows you to adjust the border width, color, and style of an element.

55

border-radius:

The border radius creates rounded corners.

57

color

"Color" is used to edit the color of a text.

45

/*comment*/

The comment is used to insert notes between the lines. Comments in *CSS* are written differently than in *HTML*. 57

display:

The display *property* defines how an element is displayed on the website. 60

flex-direction:

The flex direction defines the order in which flex elements are displayed. You can use the *values*: row, row-reverse, column, column-reverse. 68

flex-grow:

With "flex-grow" you can enlarge one or multiple flex items within a *container.* 69

float:

The float *property* is used to position and format content. For example you can float text within a *container* to the left or to the right of an image. 59

font:

The font *property* allows you to edit the font family style weight size. 46

height:

The height *property* defines the height of an element. The units: "px", "%", "vh" are the most common ones.

49

justify-content:

"Justify-content-center" is used to center the *children* of a flex element horizontally.

83

margin:

A margin is used to create space around defined borders of an element.

56

opacity

The opacity is used to adjust the transparency of an element.

61

padding:

The margin defines the space around the content, within defined borders. You can think of it like a margin inside of an element.

54

position:

The position *property* defines the way an element is positioned. The positioning is defined by the top, right, bottom and left *properties*.

57

transform:

The height *property* defines the height of an element. The units: "px", "%", "vh" are the most common ones. 49

justify-content:

"Justify-content-center" is used to center the *children* of a flex element horizontally. 83

margin:

A margin is used to create space around defined borders of an element.

56

opacity

The opacity is used to adjust the transparency of an element.

61

padding:

The margin defines the space around the content, within defined borders. You can think of it like a margin inside of an element.

54

transform:

The transform *property* applies 2D and 3D transformations on your element.

65

visibility:

The visibility defines whether an element can be seen or not. 60

width:

The width *property* defines the width of an element. The units: "px", "%", "vh" are the most common ones. 49

z-index:

You can use the z-index *property* to move an object forward in the object stack. An item with a greater z-index is displayed further forward than an item with a lower z-index.

58

Quick Reference to

Basic terms

Aos

Aos is an open source scrolling *library*. It is used to change the scrolling behavior specific elements on a website.

88

Attributes

HTML attributes provide additional information about *HTML* elements. For example the <a> *tag* uses the *href attribute* to link a URL.

Bootstrap

Bootstrap is an open source *CSS framework* for developing *responsive*, mobile first and front-end web development. It includes *CSS*- and *JavaScript*-based design templates for typography, forms, buttons, and other interface components.

47

Brackets

Brackets is a source code editor with primary focus on web development. It is written in *HTML, CSS* and *JavaScript*.

14

Child

An *HTML child* is an element that is contained within another element. The <body> *tag* can be considered the *child* of the <html> element.

Container

An *HTML container* corresponds to an element that surrounds another. The <html> *tag* is the *container* of the <head> and <body> *tags*.

CSS

CSS stands for *Cascading Style Sheets*. It is used for the presentation of an *HTML* document.

41

Declaration

A *CSS declaration* consists of a *property* and of a *value*. For example "color: red" is considered as a *declaration*.

44

Fancybox

FancyBox is a tool for displaying images, and multi-media content *responsively* in a Mac-style that floats overtop of web page.

89

JavaScript

JavaScript enables interactive web pages. It is an essential part of websites and web applications.

jQuery

jQuery is a *JavaScript library* to simplify *JavaScript* procedures. Since May 2019, *jQuery* has been used by 73% of the 10 million most popular websites.

Parent

An *HTML parent* is an element that contains another element. The <html> *tag* is the *parent* of the <body> *tag*.

Property

A *CSS property* is the first part of a *CSS declaration*. For example "color", "font" or "back-ground" are properties.

44

Pseudo-Classes

A *pseudo-class* is used to define a special state of an element. For example, the state of a link can be hovered, visited or active.

62

Pseudo-Elements

Pseudo-elements can be used to edit parts of an element. For example, it can be used to edit the first line, first letter or last letter of an element. 62

Responsive

A *responsive* website is a website designed for both desktops and mobile devices.

Selector

A *CSS selector* is used to select the *HTML* element which is to be edited. *Tag* names, classes and IDs can be used as *selectors*. 44

Slicknav

Slicknav is a *JavaScript library* used to create *responsive* navigation bars. 90

Tag

HTML tags are hidden keywords within a web page that determine how your web browser must format and display the content. Most *HTML tags* have an opening and a closing *tag*. 18

Value

A *CSS value* is the second half of a *declaration*. For example "red", "green" or "blue", "12px" or "inherit" could be *values*. 44

Variable

A *value* that may take on more than one *value* during the runtime of a program.

Index

A

B

C

D

F

H

I

U

V

W

Z

www.ingramcontent.com/pod-product-compliance
Lightning Source LLC
LaVergne TN
LVHW051926160726
843515LV00014B/2676/J
* 9 7 8 2 4 9 2 2 8 0 0 0 9 *